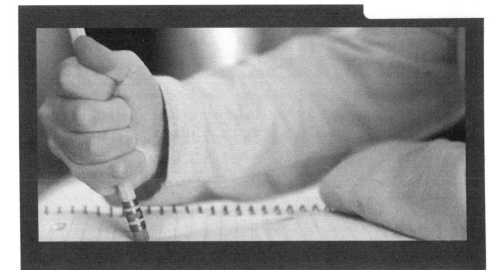

Homeschooling Your Child

With Special Needs

Practical Encouragement and Support for
Learning with Differences

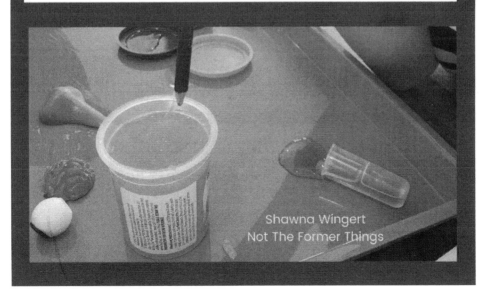

Shawna Wingert
Not The Former Things

Table of Contents

Forward by *Shawna Wingert*
Creator of *Not the Former Things* and *Different by Design Learning*

Part One: The Basics

Part Two: The Reality

Part Three: The Basics

About the Author

Forward

It happens almost every day.

I hear from a mom desperate for information on homeschooling her child with special needs and learning differences.

She is terrified. She's been told to not even consider it - that the experts need to be the ones in charge of her child's special education.

She's terrified, yes. But somewhere, deep down, she knows it's not working. She knows there just has to be another way.

I am writing this book for her, for you, and for the mom I was almost a decade ago, as we began our homeschooling journey. This is exactly the book I would've loved to read as we began.

Special thanks to my sweet boys for so many years of life and learning right alongside one another. They have been the catalyst for so much joy and passion in my life. Plus, they both seem to have inherited my sense of humor and sarcasm, so I think my work here is just about done.

Part One: The Basics

"The best teachers are those who show you where to look, but don't tell you what to see." - Alexandra K. Tenfor

Chapter 1: Our Story

When I was a little girl, I wanted to be a teacher.

I loved the idea of being the one directing a classroom. I wanted to be the one behind the desk, grading papers. I wanted to have children hug my legs and give me apples. I wanted to write on chalkboards, create seasonally themed bulletin boards, and administer spelling tests.

When I was twenty years old, I found myself beginning the student teaching process. I was now an Education major at the university, with an emphasis in Special Education. I had completed all of my in-class preparation, and it was time to finally be able to put into practice all I had learned. I arrived early, on my very first day in the first-grade classroom, feeling confident and excited. I left that day certain that I had made a mistake.

Teaching was a lot less about me than I had imagined. Teaching, I quickly learned, was about the students and their needs. The needs in that little classroom were so numerous that I felt I simply couldn't keep up. Moreover, my heart felt like it was breaking all day long because I couldn't give the children the time and attention they seemed to require.

My education degree helped me become, not a teacher, but a very successful training and development consultant. For ten years, I have worked all over the country for various fortune 500 companies, developing learning plans for employee development. After that, I worked with smaller businesses, defining business plans that leveraged people and their strengths as a business's number one asset.

I was good at what I did, mostly because of my teaching background. Whereas businesses usually looked at operations and processes first, I worked to help businesses see the potential that was right in front of them – their employees. Time and time again, I saw businesses succeed against all odds, because of the attention they paid to individualized, employee development.

I loved my job. I was well compensated. It was challenging work, and it required only my professional, logical side. It did not require any part of my heart, and I liked it that way.

Then, I became a mom. Twice. Two little boys that each stole a piece of my heart that I didn't know existed. Two little boys that required more care than I ever thought I could possibly give.

I pulled my oldest son out of public school at the end of second grade After two years, it was clear that although he was in the top 1% of second graders in the school district and had perfect grades, he was miserable every single day (and therefore so was I). It was also painfully clear that, because he was so advanced academically, he was not learning anything new at all.

It took seeing him painfully try to fit in, hearing kids tease him about his 6th grade reading level, having meltdowns every morning over having to put on shoes and getting out the door, his teacher telling me that she didn't need my input, the constant threat of bells ringing, crowded cafeterias, PE on the prickly grass...it took all of this to cause me to take a step back and say, maybe this isn't working.

Making the decision to homeschool was difficult for me.

I went to school to be a teacher. I *loved* school myself. But I also knew that my son, and his little brother, were not loving it - not even a little. Their experiences seemed to be polar opposites of my own.

I saw their differences. I heard the bullies making fun. I felt the frustration of their teachers, trying to do the best they could for all 30 of their children, but not able to really devote too much time and attention to anyone.

After years of asking for help from doctors, teachers, and psychologists, to figure out why my children could not function in a mainstream classroom, we decided to eliminate the classroom. My youngest son finished preschool, but never saw the inside of a kindergarten classroom. My oldest packed up his desk on the last day of the second grade and never returned.

A year later, my oldest son was diagnosed with autism and generalized anxiety disorder. He also scored in the genius range on the IQ test.
It all began to make sense.

A year after that, we learned that my youngest son is profoundly dyslexic and has a significant processing delay. He too scored in the genius range on the IQ test. More pieces of our education puzzle began to fall into place. Two years later, we found ourselves back in a doctor's office this time receiving chronic illness diagnoses for my oldest son. And the next three years brought more diagnoses for my youngest son.

Almost all of the children in that first classroom I found myself student teaching in twenty years ago, fell into one or more of my children's diagnostic categories. It is abundantly clear, that God has been preparing me to be a special education teacher all along.

This is what I have learned along the way.

Chapter 2: Is it OK to Use The Term "Special Needs?"

People can be really mean sometimes.

People can be really kind sometimes.

This pretty much sums up what I have learned about the internet as a blogger.

I delete inappropriate comments without responding. I try to help anyone who seems like they may need it and I hope to communicate how grateful I am for the massive support and encouragement I feel from you, my gracious readers.

But every once in a while, there's a comment that I just can't shake. Like the time someone said I was prostituting my sons. Or the time someone said I should've done the world a favor and not had children. These types of comments require time for me to calm down and gain some perspective. (It's a part of the blogging experience. Period. I get it.)

Recently, I came across a comment that was not overtly mean. It did not threaten my children or call me a bad mom. But it has been hard for me to let go.

The comment?

> "You say special needs way too much. You are labeling your poor children when you do that and it's not fair. You should say differently-abled or something."

I understand the intent (although, for the record, I think judging is never a good way to inspire change) and it got me thinking.

Is it OK to use the term "special needs" when referring to my children, or any child for that matter?

The definition of *special needs* is, according to Google Dictionary –

"Particular educational requirements resulting from learning difficulties, physical disability, or emotional and behavioral difficulties."

Special needs is a term that originated in the educational system to denote children that literally had "special" or unique education requirements.

I could argue that all children, when we look at them as individuals, have special or unique educational requirements and that part of motherhood is figuring them out – but I won't.

The truth is, I just don't have the energy to worry about all of this.

Whether or not the needs are special, my children have needs that require a lot of me.

Call it want you want.

My desire is to encourage and support moms, no matter what the needs of their children, and communicate that we are not alone in this. I try to do this with every single post. I also want to make you laugh if I can, to make up for the seriousness of it all.

That's it.

In order to achieve this, I have to find language that makes sense and can be easily understood by all of us.

Special needs is a catch-all that I use to define the differences in my boys' bodies and in our lives.

I do not see it as derogatory, although I know it can be and is used in derogatory ways by some.

The words themselves are never the problem. It's the heart and intent behind them.

For example, Mother Teresa, referred to the developmentally disabled and mentally ill as "mental."

No matter what she called them, she served and loved a typically shunned group of people without bias. Her heart was pure, even if her words might have been construed as offensive.

Yes, words matter. I would never want to communicate that I think otherwise. Often, I receive emails from adults on the spectrum that have concerns about the language used or references made to mothering a child with autism. As a matter of practice, I typically delete anything that could potentially be offensive.

Why?

Because I am not on the spectrum. I cannot possibly tell an autistic adult what they should and should not be comfortable with – in fact, I hope they tell me so that I can better understand.

I am however, most assuredly a mother of children with special needs, no matter what we call them.

Used in the right context, I think it is the best description.

My children are both comfortable with "special needs" and don't connect it to any judgement. My youngest has even used it to describe the pets he wants to adopt.

"I want to help all the animals that have special needs and need me to give them special care."

I love this.

For my sweet boy, special needs immediately denotes care, not an assessment of ability.

It with this in mind that I have included "special needs" in the title of this book. I also use it throughout. I mean no disrespect.

It's simply the best term I know to accurately portray all that we have going on in our homeschool.

Part Two: The Reality

"Little things are indeed little, but to be faithful in little things
is a great thing." - Mother Teresa

Chapter 3: Am I Qualified to Homeschool My Child with Special Needs?

"Aren't you worried that you are keeping him from really getting the help he needs?"

"You don't want your son to miss out on the professional help the school system provides."

"How can you possibly think that you are more qualified than someone who has been trained to help with autism and dyslexia?"

All three of these comments were made by other moms, concerned about my ability to appropriately homeschool my boys. All three caused me a little bit of anxiety. A little bit of fear. And then a whole lot of I just wish they could see how good this has been for my boys, how much progress they've made, how much this adds to their life (and mine).

We have been homeschooling now for more than eight years.

We began before we had a single diagnosis for either child.

After two years in public school classrooms, it was clear that although he was in the top 1% of second graders in the school district, my son was miserable every single day. Because he was so advanced academically, he was also not being challenged by the curriculum and was not truly learning. The sensory issues my son deals with every day, are alone enough to make schooling at home a good choice for him. He could hear other student's pencils writing on papers in classrooms, the whir of the air conditioner, the ticking of the clock. He could smell the sickly, sweet lunchboxes in the corner after lunch, the grass on the bottom of someone's shoe, the markers used on the dry erase board.

My son's memories of school mostly revolve around the sensory overload he experienced every single day.

When we finally received medical and neuro-psychological evaluations and diagnoses, I was repeatedly asked if I would be putting the boys back in school.

My answer was a very resolved, "No."

One of the reasons I am so passionate about writing about homeschooling is because I think there is a serious misconception that homeschooling is not a viable option when your child has special needs. Moreover, there is also a perception that a child with special needs is missing out on valuable therapies and resources when they are not a part of the school system.

The question I am most often asked in relation to homeschooling with special needs is this - Am I Qualified to Homeschool My Children with Special Needs?

My answer is, in short, "Yes."

The longer, more detailed response always includes these four points.

1. Because I Actually Went to School to be a Special Education Teacher I Have Some Idea of What Traditional Schooling Would Be Like for My Boys

I did my student teaching in special education classrooms. I studied book upon book about individualized learning plans, IEP's, education law, and classroom management.

I know that for my two boys and their needs, there is no way a traditional classroom would be an option.

Both of my children have genius level IQs, but also have serious education deficits. This asynchrony makes classroom placement difficult.

For example, at home, my dyslexic thirteen-year old is reading at a 2nd grade level, but is completing 10th grade level science and history. This would be impossible to replicate in a school environment.

(Please note: In my state, no special training or education level is required at all to homeschool any child, including those with special needs. Some states do require a little more oversight, but *all* allow parents to choose to homeschool their children, no matter what the diagnosis. I have some education and training, but it is not necessary or required.)

2. My Children Have Access to Therapists and Services

My children do use outside resources (boy do they). For example, my youngest saw an educational therapist for more than a year to help lay the groundwork for reading. In addition, I met with her once a month and she taught me the methods she used with him, so that I could replicate them at home.

The same is true for occupational therapy and social skills therapies for my oldest. We are by no means doing this alone and have plenty of experts helping to influence my children's overall development.

3. Every Single Mom I Know with Unique Little Ones Like Mine Is an Expert

I say this with complete confidence. We read more books, learn more online, ask more questions, and try to piece together answers for our children beyond what the school system can provide. Children with special needs, whether in school or not, rely on their parents to be their most passionate advocates. This is true in IEP meetings, doctors' appointments, therapists' offices, and parent-teacher conferences, without fail.

It is also true in homeschooling. I know my boys better than anyone else on the planet. I know what works and what doesn't work like when my oldest did not sleep and was anxious all night long. I know how difficult the last set of sight words were for my youngest, and can take the time to research the best way to help him proceed. I have the time and the passion that would be unrealistic to expect anything from anyone else. You do too.

4. This Is the Best Choice for My Family

I care deeply about my children's education. I have put a lot of thought into this. What I have found is that homeschooling is the best way to give them what they need to be successful in life. This is true academically, as well as socially. We have a supportive and loving community of friends who also homeschool. My children benefit from the opportunity to make friends in their own time and at their own pace, as much as they benefit from progressing academically at their own pace. Homeschooling actually gives them a social experience that makes sense for their needs.

The longer we do this, the more progress I see, and the more I learn that I am perfectly qualified to homeschool my children with special needs.

So are you.

Chapter 4: Getting Started

My first day of homeschooling was amazing. The second day was positively awful. Every day since has been somewhere in between.

And so it goes....

I was over-prepared for all the wrong things when we began homeschooling. The bookshelves were tidy, the curriculum was perfectly planned, and the crafts were ready to go that first day.

What I lacked was perspective.

I spent most of that first year frustrated and tired.

We were headed towards a diagnosis, I knew it at that point, but I still found myself trying to recreate the very school environment that had been such a disaster for my children.

Getting started was daunting. I wanted to quit more times than I can count. I hid in the bathroom and cried big tears more days than not. To this day, I am still 100% sure that I am messing this up.

Eight years later though, I can tell you that it has all been worth it.

These two truths are what I wish someone would have shared with me as we were getting started.

1. *You Are Not Alone in Doubting Your Abilities*

If you have considered this option for your child, but are worried that you won't be able to do it well, you are not alone.

Every single mom I know who is homeschooling her children has exactly this same fear. And every single one of their children, are learning and thriving.

Like anything else with our children, there are some things we just have to figure out as we go. Homeschooling is like that, only with field trips and clay.

2. Make Learning about Your Children Your First Priority

This will save you so much time, effort and frustration. I made the mistake initially, of thinking that my boys would need to get used to me being their teacher. I was wrong. I found that in order to really be able to accommodate their unique needs, I needed to learn as much as possible about them!

Here are some examples of what I have come to know about my children, and now this information informs our homeschooling.

For My Youngest Son, Slow is Fast.

He processes information about 30% slower than the average and has profound learning differences that affect his ability to read, spell and write. He also happens to be highly gifted and have reasoning abilities that were off the charts in his evaluation.

These unique qualities now color almost everything I do in educating him, particularly how I pace his learning. For example, he is still not able to spell, or even consistently read basic sight words. We worked on the word "the" for almost three full years.

We have done flashcards, written copy work, spelled with blocks, numerous worksheets, countless read alouds, and even made up our own song (t-h-e spells "the"). He still doesn't recognize some of the most basic words right away. You can imagine that this can be frustrating, and it is – both for me and especially for him.

My son knows he should know it, but he just can't retrieve the information from his complicated little brain.

In his case, slower is better.

This is why, in the long run it is actually faster.

Trying to force my son to "get it", or just skipping to the next topic because I just can't take reviewing the same thing again and again, in the long run means he learns less. I have found that praying for patience, trying to find a new approach (Honey, let's try writing "the" in shaving cream over and over again on the shower wall today) and just accepting that this is the speed that is right for him, allows him to progress at his own pace, in a meaningful way.

Conversely, the other day he solved one of his older brother's math word problems in his head. When things are read aloud, and he can just focus on the details of an equation or a problem to be solved, he is ridiculously brilliant. So, I read everything to him. His math book, his science lesson, history, Harry Potter books, books about animals, the scientific method and how to build perfect paper airplanes.

He recently picked up a book about Leonardo da Vinci, who it is rumored was dyslexic himself, and asked me to read it to him. He then proceeded to discuss the more complicated aspects of the machines good old Leo designed. He can pick up the information quickly, but it requires quite a lot of time to carefully read every single thing to him, all day long. It works because again, although it may seem slow to me, he learns rapidly and beyond grade level with this approach.

For my Oldest Son, More is More.

My two boys could not be more different. As I said above, for my youngest, less information is better. For my oldest, there are not enough books on the planet to keep him occupied and learning.

An exceptionally fast reader, he retains more detailed information from what he reads, than seems possible for a human being that is not also half computer. He collects and categorizes information as if there is a Dewey Decimal system in his brain.

He reads, on average, between 30-45 books a month (not joking and yes, that is more than one per day), most of them non-fiction. He can tell you almost anything you want to know about chemistry, every single detail of Greek Mythology, The Revolutionary War, WWII, and even parts of nuclear physics.

He knows just the entire world map, including every country, most major cities and even key exports and notable historic moments in various areas of the world. He knows all of this, because we allow him to focus almost all of his school day on reading (devouring) books, watching educational YouTube videos and then discussing them with him afterwards.

The two things he struggles with most, are holding a pencil and math. Holding a pencil is a very big deal for my son. Because his hands are such an affected part of his sensory processing disorder, it is extremely uncomfortable for him to write anything – even to practice signing his name. I allow him to type just about everything, but part of his school day includes an attempt at practicing signing his name, as if he needed to write a check or secure a contract.

I say "attempt" because some days, this is just too much for him and he literally cannot do it no matter how hard he tries. I try not to freak out about his future (where I imagine him making X's on all legal documents), and he does his best to practice on days when he is feeling less overstimulated.

Math has also been a struggle – largely because it is difficult to learn math through simply reading and accumulating information. What has been helpful for us is including the second set of books in a series called *Life of Fred*. These books tell a story and incorporate advanced math into the plot as a way to learn concepts.

Turns out, he learns very well this way, and has started giving me algebraic equations to solve while we drive. (He can now easily do algebra, but still has to use a calculator for basic multiplication – ah the joys of asynchronous learning.)

Paying close attention to what naturally works and what does not work, allows me to better educate my children. It also makes learning much more fun and me a lot less stressed. If you are just getting started, please let me encourage you.

You can do this. Let your child teach you how he or she needs to learn.

And one more time...you *can* do this.

Chapter 5: Expectations vs. Reality

"I think you might be losing sight of the fact that he has an autism spectrum diagnosis. That's not going away. We need to talk about adjusting your expectations."

I distinctly remember my son's developmental pediatrician saying this in an appointment about a year after his diagnosis.

She said it in response to me telling her all the things we were "working on" and all the things that were not going well and all the meltdowns that we wish weren't part of our life. The week prior to the appointment had not been a great one.

I started off feeling totally overwhelmed by what I perceived as the lack of progress in our life. My son's sensory system was a jangled mess and his younger brother not reading the word "the" (again) was enough to make me want to go back to bed.

Add to that a major meltdown that erupted in actual punches being thrown at his brother in the post office, plus the lady with way too much make-up that made a very rude comment, and I was certain I had completely failed us - again. I went to bed praying for direction and order and peace.

The next day, we had a follow-up appointment with his developmental pediatrician. God has perfect timing.

When the doctor asked my son to leave the room, I thought she was going to tell me all the things we needed to do next. Instead, she basically said my expectations didn't match my reality.

My son has Autism. He has severe sensory processing issues that aggravate an already pervasive anxiety disorder.

He *will* have meltdowns. Period.
He *will* perseverate on topics for days and weeks at a time. Period.

He *will* struggle with his body and balance and social function.
Period.

Apparently, years later, I am still struggling to fully accept all of
this.

Even a year in, I still needed the doctor to confirm a diagnosis
that I could so plainly see right in front of me.

And her doing so was an absolute blessing.

I walked out of her office in tears...tears of relief and gratitude.
I spent the rest of the week focused on how best to help and
love and accept my son, right where he is.
Actually, I spent the rest of the week focused on how best to
help and love and accept my life, right where it is.

Expectations, ones that do not match my reality, are
suffocating.
Maybe you have encountered this as well? The should's. The
what-if's. The why's.

Please don't misunderstand, we should work on making progress. And I was reminded that we have made progress, a ton of it actually.

When I first walked into that office, I was terrified. My son hadn't slept in weeks. He was harming himself, and me, every single day.

I had forgotten how far we've come.

When my expectations don't match my reality, we all lose. Expectations are like that - I get so focused on how I think things should be, that I lose sight of how wonderful they already are.

One year later, he was sleeping all the way through the night (well, most of the time). We could actually leave the house and not worry about someone getting hurt in the car. He hadn't hurt himself in months. He hadn't hurt me in even longer.

If you had told me a year prior to that appointment that our current reality is what I could look forward to, I would've rejoiced and cried tears of joy.

That day and almost every day since, I have tried to remind myself of this simple fact.

Rather than thinking about when things will change, I want to live my life, love my kids and pursue their education exactly as we are today.

Chapter 6: Sleep Matters

This morning was a tough one.

I was up until almost 4:00 AM with my son. In the haze of perseverating chatter about computer builds and salt water tanks, I was struck at around 3:00 AM, by how little my life has changed.

It's been thirteen years since my son was a newborn, and yet many nights feel exactly the same. Sleeping for short stretches, only to be awakened by the needs of a child I love dearly who just is not equipped to sleep, is a constant in my life. Mothering a child with special needs can be so, so tiring. Literally. So tiring.

Studies suggest that nearly 80% of children with autism and other special needs have sleep problems.

This means that 80% of parents with children with autism and other special needs also have sleep problems.

It is a very real, very present reality for many of us. And, in my experience, one that most doctors and therapists cannot really identify with.

"Make sure you cut out any sugar and electronics for at least three hours before bedtime," was the constant recommendation when my son was younger. It was infuriating. We had been doing that for years, with absolutely no effect.

Sleeping for very short periods of time, only to be wakened again and again is used as torture in some countries. I for one, would like to say I understand why.

And my son is just as tired. The years of not sleeping well take their toll. One of the greatest benefits of homeschooling for us has been the ability to accommodate sleep disturbances.

If my youngest son is anxious until 2:30 AM, I can allow him to sleep in a bit the next morning instead of waking him for the 7:30 AM bus. If my oldest wakes for the day at 3:30 AM, I can change our plan for the day to include more relaxed and less strenuous activities and learning. If both of them are awake off and on all night (and they often are), I can choose to turn on documentaries and take a nap on the couch for a few hours in the afternoon.

This may seem basic, and I guess it is. But it's true. Sleep, and the lack thereof, makes a significant difference in our children's ability to learn and retain information.

Working with my sons' natural sleep patterns, instead of constantly fighting against them has lessened the constant stress bedtimes and wake times once caused us.

If your family struggles with consistent sleep, like mine, I want to encourage you to view accommodating your child's sleep needs as part of your family's educational plan - because it absolutely affects our children's learning and and our own teaching.

Chapter 7: Life Skills

My son showed me exactly how he planned to install a CPU into his computer yesterday. If you don't know what that is, don't worry. You are in good company. I listen to my son tell me all about computer parts for most of the day, every day, and I am still not 100% sure I know what it really is.

He walked me through step by step, in painstaking detail, not only how to install it, but how the actual device functions. The way it communicates, what one set of cords does vs. the other, why the motherboard goes in this spot, and so many more things that I completely did not understand.

I sat there in awe, so proud of the man he is becoming. He is realizing his strengths, and using them to compensate for the aspects of his life that are difficult. It is exactly what he has been working towards for almost seven years now.

And, honestly, I couldn't help but feel a pang of confusion and disbelief. He can do all of this - but he may not be able to navigate dinner tonight.

It's something I don't think we talk about as much as we should. A child with special needs often masters things are that outrageously difficult for a typical individual - sometimes even impossible. Never being taught to build a computer, and yet being able to do just that is a small example.

But it's the basics that are difficult. Eating. Sleeping. Drinking Water. Shopping. Taking Medicines. Showering. Getting Dressed. Playing.

These are the areas of my son's life that are the most complicated. They are also the areas of my mothering that are the most challenging.

They happen every single day, all day.

Eating and sleeping are basic life requirements, and yet they are, without a doubt, the most challenging aspects of my son's life.

"I'm hungry, but I can't eat."
"I'm tired, but I can't sleep."
"I want to go to the store and look at air fresheners, but I can't be in the store."

He has learned to better communicate what is happening. And it's so helpful. Verbally being able to say I can't do something is a big deal around here.

And I am grateful for it. And it is exhausting.

This is an example of an average day mothering my son through the basics of his life:

Morning

He didn't want breakfast at 9:00 AM. It's now 10:00 AM. Time to try again. Nope. OK. I will ask again at 10:30 AM and this time I will offer bagels and cream cheese. That's soft, it might work. Good, bagels and cream cheese it is. Except, no. He took one bite and gagged. OK, scrambled eggs worked. Now we can get his medicines prepped. He said he would take them in an hour - he just can't right now with the taste of egg in his mouth. I need to set an alarm so I don't forget. 11:45 AM and meds are down.

Afternoon

It's 2:00 PM and he wants to go to the pet store. I need him to eat something first. The pet store is usually OK, but the lighting and smells can be weird, and we have had meltdowns there before. Deep breath. It's 2:30 PM and I am making a turkey sandwich. One of his favorites. We should be good to go.

Evening

It's dinner time and he wants to eat in his room again. There are studies that show families that eat at the table together do well. But he hates the feeling of the chair on his hip. And he can't stand the sound of his brother chewing, or tapping his feet on the floor, or both. Am I a bad mom for just letting him eat the flippin' lasagna alone? At least he is eating. I am going to let it go. We are getting close to bedtime and I am thinking through how to help him shower. The smell of teenage boy is real. I know it's tough for him, but we gotta do it. He balks. Shoot. I decide to entice him with the brand new items we bought at Lush. Maybe the shower gel will be my friend right now. He is seriously not going to do it. He says it is just too much tonight and that he promises to shower tomorrow. I decide to respect his wishes. He is communicating how he feels. That is progress. We have nothing planned outside of our house tomorrow. It should be calmer. He should be able to keep that promise.

The Middle of the Night

It's 1:30 AM and he is still up. He wants to sleep. It's obvious that he is tired. But he just can't. I ask him if he wants to talk to me a little, just to get drowsy. He does. I feel my eyelids closing every once in a while, but for the most part, I am pleased that he is so calm. Instead of getting anxious he is settling down. By 2:15 AM, he is asleep. By 2:16 AM, so am I.

Our life necessarily looks different.

My son spends more time learning the basics, like eating and hygiene, than he ever will in subjects like science and math. And I am 100% OK with it.

What makes it complicated is the rest of the world.

Not understanding, assuming he is spoiled, questioning why I allow him to make the decision instead of just demanding obedience. Too often, my son is questioned by doctors, by other kids, and even his brother, as to why he just can't take the meds, eat the food, or go to the store.

He doesn't have an answer to these questions. If he did, we wouldn't be spending so much time on these things.

Too often, I am also questioned by the well-meaning specialist, by a mom who doesn't know us very well, by my youngest son. But I have an answer. Everyone is different. Everyone has strengths and weaknesses. My son is stronger in his strengths than any other teenager I know. He also works harder, every single day, on the things that are tough for him.

Sometimes the basics are the most difficult.

Sometimes simple, isn't simple.

Sometimes development looks wildly different for one child vs. another. And sometimes, we just have to proceed at a pace that is right for our children.

Homeschool allows us to do just that.

I don't think the basics will ever be easy for my son. But I have seen enough progress to know that he will eventually figure out how to best approach eating, sleeping and shopping. Until then, I will help him.

We incorporate life skills into our days as if they were an algebra class or language arts program. It's a basic premise, but one that I think we often overlook as parents homeschooling children with special needs.

Please let me encourage you – many special education programs in traditional schools often incorporate life skills such as grocery shopping, cooking, and navigating bus schedules. You are doing the exact same thing when you are working with your little one on brushing her teeth. It counts. Not only as parenting, but as education.

Part Three: The Basics

"ABC. Easy as One, two, three. Or simple as Do re mi, ABC, one, two, three, baby, you and me." - Jackson 5

Chapter 8: Feeling the Pressure to Recreate School

I had a school room with a lovely, perfectly organized set of books, curriculum, and manipulatives. I had a bell, all set and ready to ring for start time, break time, and lunch time. It was going to be amazing.

And it was. For exactly one day.

Then reality of homeschooling hit. My children did not do well in a school environment. It was one of the reasons they were no longer going to school. So why was I trying to recreate that exact environment in our home?

There are so many ways that this has played out in the past nine years.

Like the time I was convinced that my sons needed to be in classes at least one day a week, so that they could be social and learn from a better teacher than me.

Let me just repeat what I already wrote: A school environment did not work well for my children. It was obvious. But I am a slow learner, and apparently really like spending money on registration fees and classes that we will only attend for approximately two weeks until I remember why we pulled them out of school and homeschool in the first place.

Or the time I thought I really needed to add knitting and crochet to our curriculum. (Because that is what every prepubescent, special needs child needs – to try desperately to complete a fine motor skill task that even his mom can't do.)

Or the time I was sure that if we started school every day by 8:30 a.m., we would somehow be more focused and actually learn all the things. I am sad to say that the person who has learned the most in this homeschooling journey, especially when it comes to helping my children academically, is me.

Recreating a school environment just doesn't work for my children. Maybe it doesn't for yours either.

I will share what does work in coming chapters, but for right now, I just want to encourage you that it is OK for your homeschool to look different - not only from a traditional school environment, but also from a traditional homeschool environment.

Nontraditional learners require a nontraditional approach. You are not doing it wrong. You are not messing it up. You are simply figuring out what works best for your children.

Chapter 9: The Pros and Cons of Homeschooling Children with Special Needs

Homeschooling a child with special needs is not what I thought it would be.

It's so much better and in some ways, worse.

When my son was in public school, I spent a lot of time daydreaming about what it would be like if I could stay home with him and homeschool.

No drop-off meltdowns.

No calls from the teacher.

No sinking feeling at pick-up time, seeing the other boys making fun of his shoes.

The thought that I might be able to bring him home and make it better haunted me. Then, at the end of second grade, we did it.

We began homeschooling.

Eight plus years later, I can say with absolute certainty that it was the right decision for my family.

But, looking back, I also realize that my assumption that homeschooling would "fix" it all was way, way off.

With that in mind, I want to share an honest look at, what I consider to be, the pros and cons specific to homeschooling children with special needs.

The Pros

A Focus On Strengths

One of the greatest pros is that homeschooling allows us to focus on and build upon my children's strengths, rather than remediating weaknesses. This approach helps build confidence and over time, my sons have been better able to perform in all areas.

Decreased Anxiety

Both of my sons have anxiety disorder diagnoses. Both are significantly less anxious because we homeschool. My oldest's explosive behavior decreased significantly when we removed the daily expectation that he function in a school environment.

Quality Social Opportunities

Although one of the main criticisms of homeschooling is that it decreases a child's opportunity for socialization, the truth is that for my kids, homeschooling has allowed for better social opportunities than school ever provided.

First, no bullies. Second, when they meet a friend, they have time to work through any social discomfort in a relaxed environment. Moreover, my children have friends that have stayed friends for years. They have grown together, worked through differences together and developed deeper relationships than a 20 minute recess could ever provide.

I have shared, time and time again, about the benefits of homeschooling my children with special needs. In fact, I have an entire post that lists 101 reasons why it works for us.

The Cons

Although I have shared a lot about the benefits, this is the first time I have created a list of things that are actually more difficult because of our decision to homeschool, particularly with my children's special needs.

Lack of Daily Structure

As much as I try to create a **routine and structure** to our days, there is simply no way I can offer the same level of predictability in our home that a formal school setting offers.

Because children on the spectrum and with mood disorders thrive and often demand a level of structure beyond what homeschooling provides, this is a con that must be noted and considered. I believe my youngest would, in fact, benefit from the daily predictability that school provides.

Outside Resources

Every single outside resource we employ operates with a school mindset. Doctors and therapists are trained to help school age kids in ways that include the school environment. Even some diagnoses require an assessment of school ability and social/behavioral performance in order to diagnose. I can't tell you how many doctors have looked at the parent assessment and teacher assessment forms and struggled to figure out which one to give me.

The truth is, our world assumes a typical school experience for children. Most professionals are not sure what to do with a child who is homeschooled.

I'm exhausted.

Because I am their teacher, mom, and even therapist most days, I am tired. I am overworked and have very little time for outside interests.

One of my son's therapists once asked him what his mom's hobbies were and he, looking puzzled, answered, "Doing the dishes?" A realistic look at the pros and cons of homeschooling would be incomplete without this very present reality.

After looking at the pros and cons for my family, I find, over and over again, that the benefits far outweigh the costs. Although I realize that, in some areas, a formal school might better meet our needs, when I look at the entire picture I can easily see that homeschooling allows the type of childhood that I want for my children, and even the type of motherhood I crave for myself.

I have learned that there is no perfect solution and all educational options have their own lists of pros and cons. This is the very best decision I can possibly make for my children, and that makes the costs well worth it.

Chapter 10: Screen Time – The Good, the Bad, and the Ugly

The week I wrote this chapter happened to be our "Screen-Free" week. Or around here, "Feel Like A Bad Mom" week.

When I think about the amount of time my children spend on screens, my head hurts. The guilt. The assurance that I am absolutely doing the wrong thing. The feeling that good moms would never do the things I do.

The truth is, I sometimes hate screen time. I see the effect it has been known to have on my children and others. I also see the effect that getting outside, being in nature, and just moving has on my children and others.

So why do I allow it, more than the average mom even?

Because the truth is, there are real, very tangible benefits to "screen time" that matter more to me than the detriments. I know this is not a popular, or even widely held view. In fact, I am a little nervous to even include this chapter in my book.

But every year, the dreaded "Screen Free Week" happens, and every year I freak out about it, feel guilty, and we fail the screen free test miserably.

This year, I have decided instead, to acknowledge and intentionally define why our family has chosen a different screen time path.

My Family Has Unique Educational Needs that Make Screen Time a Fabulous Tool

My oldest son has autism and massive anxiety that is exacerbated by sensory processing issues. The best way for him to learn anything is in complete silence. Even the sound of another person's pencil on a piece of paper is enough to cause major stress and drama. Even my voice can ring in his ears after just a very short lesson.

But watching a quick YouTube video on Peru for example, and then finding various websites to research and learn about said subject is much more effective. This has made my son a serious expert in all things Peruvian, including native plants, animals, topography, geography, different cultures within Peru, travel and tourism, and more.

Because he could do it at his own pace, and in a way that works well with his sensory needs, the iPad has acted as his primary teacher for all of this, with me merely checking in from time to time to see how he is doing. His recent country report is wonderful and he completed the report in PowerPoint, without my help. Yet another screen, yet another advantage for him.

This same child also has an auto-immune disorder that creates massive joint and nerve pain, making him sometimes so fatigued that he literally cannot get out of bed. On the bad days, he still completes some "learning". I lie down with him, and we watch YouTube videos together. Is it ideal? No. But it keeps him engaged on days that are so very tough for him, physically and emotionally.

My youngest son, of course, has a different set of educational needs.
He has profound dyslexia, ADHD, and a processing disorder. He is on screens much less, but mostly because he is naturally a very active child. He enjoys everything about the outdoors and given the choice, would much rather put down the iPad, and go out and bounce on the trampoline.

Still, Minecraft has been a very effective tool to help him with spelling and reading. We use it to practice typing sentences and commands. He thinks he is merely playing a game, but I see the progress he makes when he is not so anxious about his lack of reading ability.

For my youngest, I find I am actually intentionally finding ways to incorporate screens into his schooling. Educational apps and learning games are age appropriate for my almost teenager barely reading at a second grade level. Books are still a part of his learning, of course, but as I have mentioned, most in his reading level are babyish and dull. They cause so much more self-doubt and anxiety than any screen ever could.

There Are Very Few People Who Can Easily Babysit My Boys

This may be a selfish benefit, but a screen time benefit just the same.

With my children's unique needs, there are only a handful of people we know who can handle them well. And when we *do* get someone to watch them, it's so we can go out for the evening, or get much needed errands done.

The truth is, sometimes, screens help me get the laundry folded in peace. Sometimes, they keep my youngest safe and distracted when his older brother is violently melting down. Sometimes, they let me take a quick nap when I have been up since 3:30 in the morning with an anxiety ridden child. It's not ideal, but it works and we are all better because of it.

We Do Have Limits, but Only on When to Take Breaks and on Content, not Overall Time Spent on the Screen

In our family, we have specific limits on content. We do not allow mature rated video games and often talk to our boys about not electronically training their minds to be violent. We also do not allow them to speak and interact with each other any differently than they would while playing outside together. This includes language, not helping each other out, and name calling.

The boys can now recite my mantras: 'There May Be a Screen between You but Your Brother Is Still Your Brother on the Other Side' and 'Real People Matter More than the Electronic Ones'.

We also encourage frequent and regular breaks similar to what I employed when I worked in an office setting, I plan for my sons to get up and get out regularly, thereby avoiding long stretches of screen time.

Sometimes, they hurry through whatever task or outdoor activity I ask them to do. Other times, they get totally caught up in something else and do not return to the screen. Either way, this seems to dramatically lessen the wild hyperactivity or aggression that can sometimes occur from too much time spent staring at a screen.

When all is said and done, this is just what works for us. Every family is different, and I trust your decisions to be what is best for yours. Clearly my children's needs are unique, but I think in any family, being intentional about screen time can be just as beneficial as eliminating it all together.

Chapter 11: Learning to Ignore Grade Level

"He is reading at a first grade level now," I said to the doctor, holding my breath.

"What?" she said with a mix of surprise and concern. "He's ten."

I paused for a moment, and decided to ignore the comment welling up in my throat about how I am pretty sure I know how old he is.

"Well, two years ago, he was at a preschool level, so really, he has made two years' worth of progress in two years," I said, sure she would nod her head and appreciate the progress. She didn't.

We spent the rest of our time together talking about the many options for dyslexia interventions, and getting him to 'grade level'. I left feeling so sad for my youngest son, who works so hard, but never feels like it is enough. I understand why he feels this way.

Learning disabilities are so devious. His doctor is well versed in dyslexia and learning differences. She knows exactly what his IQ testing and learning profile means. She knows the asynchrony of a child profoundly gifted in some areas, and profoundly delayed in others. And she still cannot believe, after educational therapy and daily instruction for more than two years, that he is only capable of reading Dr. Seuss's Hop On Pop on his best day.

I understand why she feels this way.

We discussed the school versus homeschool options for him. I used to think he needed to be in school in order to receive the intervention he needs.

I have since learned better, but the doctor surprised me when she said, "With his needs, there is no way the school system would be able to adequately help him. You might be able to eventually get the school district to pay for him to go to special private school, but that would take years and I am not convinced it would be a good fit for him either."

"So you see my dilemma," I thought to myself, but did not say.

I came home to my children, exhausted and feeling the weight of it all.
I walked away from the appointment with good advice about all the things I need to do. I am grateful for it. And I am tired of it.

It feels like we are running some sort of race – with grade level as the finish line.

Grade level means nothing to my children.
My oldest is reading at a college level proficiency, but cannot perform sequential tasks, requiring even the most basic executive function.
My youngest is several grade levels ahead in history and science, but couldn't read the word "said" yesterday.

I cannot use grade level as the standard. I know this. And yet I long for it.

I want progress to be faster and more linear. I want grade level so much it hurts sometimes. I want to be able to say to anyone who asks, "Yes, they are at grade level," and never again have the discussion about how to speed up their progress.

I want to avoid the panic that rears its ugly head first thing in the morning and last thing at night. "Am I doing this right? What else can I do? Am I failing these children?"

My children are children. They are not math equations. They are not projects with completion dates.

As convenient as it would be for them to achieve grade level expectations, this is just simply not possible sometimes. More importantly, when I think about who they are becoming, what matters most in their lifetime, and how they will be most successful as adults, the less reading levels and math standards even matter.

So now, rather than worrying about all the progress we haven't made, I choose to focus on all that my sons have accomplished. Rather than worrying about grade levels and deficits, I choose to see the computer that my son built in less than two hours, on his own. I choose to see the book that my little guy picked up, and the true joy with which he read it, rather than the words on the cover: *Step 1 Ready to Read*.

Everyday, I will do the best that I can for these children. That means seeing them for who they are and accepting them, exactly where they are, no matter what their grade level.

I encourage you to choose the same.

Chapter 12: Out of the Box Learning for Out of the Box Kids

"I neeeeeeeeed to move around while you are reading to me, Momma. It's how I listen," my youngest child said to me, spinning in circles as I tried to get him to sit down with me on the couch and pay attention.

My then six-year-old child, who clearly had more energy than the rest of our entire family combined, wasn't telling me something new. He wasn't telling me something I hadn't read in numerous books, blogs, and research studies. In fact, in college, I spent an entire semester studying how to teach deaf children to read using movement.

I have known for years that children, especially young children, often learn best when incorporating play and movement into their educational activities. And yet it took my little boy looking me square in the eye and begging me to help him help me teach, to actually start incorporating play into our learning.

Sometimes, I really am the student in this whole homeschooling thing.

Why Does It Seem so Difficult to Make Play a Part of Learning?

For me, it has been a direct result of these three things:

1. It's Less Measurable

The truth is, a worksheet or a structured "sit down at the table and follow the lesson plan" activity is easily measured. When it is complete, it's complete. We can check it off the list and move on to the next assignment. This is reassuring to me. It means I can "prove" my children have been "taught" something. Yet the truth is, this approach is much more about me needing to feel successful than it is about them actually learning.

2. It Conflicts with My Own Learning Style

When I was a child, I was the one who truly enjoyed just sitting and reading a book. To this day, I am better able to focus if I can sit still. This is certainly not the case for my children, but I find myself falling back on my own version of how I think we should learn, over and over again.

3. *It Requires Some Planning and Intentionality*

Being able to pull off moving and play in conjunction with a lesson requires me to really think through how to modify the lesson. Because it requires extra planning, it is easier to just stick to the lesson plan as-is, instead of going rogue with our learning. It also often requires extra set-up and clean-up for that matter. So if I am already feeling behind or overwhelmed, play is often the first to go in our school routine. Although these have been real challenges for me as a momma and teacher, my goal is to provide an individualized, fun, and appropriate education for my boys. I know that movement and play help provide just that.

As time has gone on, through conversations with other mommas and just simply trial and error, I have learned a few tips that have helped incorporate more hands-on play and movement into our everyday learning.

Tip 1: Messy Is Not a Dirty Word

I have learned to not base any educational lesson planning on how much mess there will be before and after the activity. I have two boys. The state of our bathroom has proven to me over and over again that our life will involve some mess. Why should our school be any different?

My children are so much more engaged and have so much more fun when they are able to complete hands-on projects, without me freaking out over every sticky, dirty, cluttered surface the project involves. More importantly, they learn more. They are better able to recall the information we discuss as they create and they connect that information to the three dimensional activity before them. I will take sticky floors if it means the learning "sticks" as well.

Tip 2: Be Intentional and Plan for Play

For me, this looks different for each of my children. My youngest is super active, so I intentionally modify some activities to include movement. For example, when we are practicing speech sounds as part of his speech therapy, I will say a letter and then kick the ball to him. He will make the sound associated with the letter and then kick the ball back to me. I have no idea why this works for him, but it does. When he is thinking about kicking the ball, he actually is better able to articulate the sound and remembers it better in the long run.

For my oldest, this looks very different. While movement is not necessarily essential for his attention and retention, talking through what he has learned is vital. In order to help incorporate a little more fun into his learning, we have started creating "How-To" videos. He scripts his video and then records himself "teaching" whatever it is that he has learned. He feels like it is "play" and I find it a great way to check his understanding before we move on to a new topic.

My oldest also struggles with sensory processing issues. The only way to really synch up his sensory system is to get him moving. Unlike his brother, this requires a lot more effort on his part, and mine.

Completing occupational therapy at home has helped me incorporate movement into his days. Because OT has been a regular part of his life for so long, he understands it's benefits, or at the very least, knows it is not optional. For ten to twenty minutes every day, I incorporate some of his exercises from therapy into our learning.

An important element of this planning is paying attention to the unique gifts God has given each of my children and then I must be intentional about using those gifts in our learning. Play allows me to tailor our generic lessons to how each of my boys best function and succeed.

Tip 3: Movement Does Not Always Mean Lack of Attention
I wish I could take back at least half the times I have said, "You need to pay attention to Momma."

I used to think that because my boys were rolling back and forth on the floor while I read aloud, or standing while they completed a math lesson, they were not being attentive, or that someone had slipped them some sugar when I wasn't looking.

What I have learned in my years of homeschooling is this: my children are children. Hyperactive or not, movement is a part of how they interact with the world – including learning. For math drills, we jump on the trampoline. For oral quizzes on books or short stories, we take a walk. For any and all worksheets, we typically complete them on the floor instead of at the table.

The more I fight it, the less they learn. The more I encourage it, the more they learn. I wish I could say that I have got this play, move, learn thing all figured out – for my children's sake and my own! I don't though, not even close. The good news is that I am learning. Fortunately, so are my boys.

Part Four: The Practical

"The only source of knowledge is experience." - Albert Einstein

Chapter 13: What's the Best Curriculum for Children with Special Needs?

Our first year homeschooling, I actually thought very little about our curriculum. I look back now and wonder, "What in the world was I thinking?". I purchased the very first one I heard about from a friend. It had worked well for her family for a couple of years, so I figured it would for us as well.

Eight hundred dollars and a whole lot of tears (mine and my boys') later, I knew better.

I think every family needs to find the educational resources that work best for their individual needs.

I think this is exponentially true when we are homeschooling children with learning differences and special needs.

The truth is, some programs are just more effective with out-of-the box learners than others. Another truth – finding what works makes life so much easier for kids to be sure, but also for their teacher!

With that in mind, I want to share my basic approach to choosing learning materials and educational programs for my boys.

How to Choose a Curriculum for Kids with Learning Differences

Flexibility Is Critical

The very first thing I look for when considering any new program or supplemental material is how flexible the overall coursework and workflow will be. Any program that schedules lessons to a tee and has mostly worksheets with text, is just simply not going to be the best fit for my boys.

Often the Teachers Manual will give you more information about how to modify the program than the student pages. I look for things like "Additional activities for Practice" and "Extras" in the manuals – often, the additional activities end up being our primary learning.

Multi-Sensory

Finding a program with a multi-sensory approach, particularly one with **hands-on, tactile learning**, is critical for my youngest son. In order for him to truly grasp a concept, he usually needs some sort of hands-on interaction with it. The problem is that coming up with new activities and scouring Pinterest for ideas takes a ton of time. If I can find a program that already has it planned out for me, I'm in!

A Patchwork Quilt Approach

When it comes to a particular subject, I tend to find a variety of options, rather than sticking to a single program.

For example, when my son began US History last year, I selected *Beautiful Feet* for his primary learning which is a story based approach. We loved the program, and also soon added in map studies and historic coloring books to help make the learning stick. We also ended up cooking a few period specific foods and taking a field trip to a local history museum.

I call this my Patchwork Quilt for learning. It's got a lot going on, but once complete, it all works together beautifully and covers what we need it to.

While this may seem costly, the truth is, we move through a curriculum slowly when adding in so many extras. A typical year's worth of coursework may take us two years to complete, so the cost is spread out and more manageable. Also, the best thing about manipulatives and maps is that they last and can be reused again in later learning.

What Grade Level?

For any child, and particularly one with learning differences, you already know I think grade level is, at best, only a suggestion when it comes to selecting the right learning program. My boys are all over the place in terms of where they would actually "test" for typical school grades. The best way I have found to select the right level for my sons is to take a look at sample exercises typically offered by publishers on their websites.

It's Not the Boss, You Are

It's taken me years to learn this and, honestly, I am still learning it. No matter what, I am the one who decides how we use the curriculum. No book or sample schedule can define what's best for my family's progress.

When I start to feel a little nervous about how far we are straying from the initial instruction, I try to look at the end-result. Are my kids progressing? Are they learning? Are they enjoying the activities? If the answers are anywhere near yes, I'm good, no matter how far off the traditional curriculum we may be.

What's the Best Curriculum for Children with Special Needs?

This is what I wish someone would've told me that first year when it seemed like we were doomed to fail and I had no idea how to make this homeschool thing actually work for my children. I spent way too much time worrying about "doing it right" and checking all the boxes. Not only was it not serving my boys well, but none of us were having any fun at all.

It is my strong opinion that the very best curriculum for any child, and especially one with special needs, is the one that works best with his or her strengths and interests.

Loosening my curriculum expectations and allowing myself to just find the products that make sense for my learners, has lifted a huge weight off of my shoulders.

It has allowed us to latch on to learning in a way that inspires enthusiasm and brings joy.

Chapter 14: A Strength Based Homeschool - Why It Matters

Before I was a homeschooling mom, I was in corporate training and development.

I went to school to be a special education teacher, but quickly learned that the traditional classroom environment was not a good fit. It left me feeling drained and honestly, unable to really make a difference.

Eventually, I took what I had learned about teaching and applied it to the corporate world.

It surprised me how much I loved it.

At one point, I was invited to attend a training session at Gallup.

Their book, *Strengthfinders*, was already a wild success. This intensive training was all about using individual strengths to leverage their overall ability and performance. Based on a ton of research, the approach was simple: teaching to an individual's strengths, exponentially increases productivity and learner satisfaction.

The research also surprisingly showed that a learner, when allowed to progress in a 'strengths based' approach, increased his overall capabilities and performance, even in the areas that were weaknesses.

After completing the training, I saw the research prove itself in my own work again and again in a corporate setting. When a learner is offered to the opportunity to focus on and really use their strengths, their overall performance improves.

Fast forward a decade.

I am home now. I traded that world of pretty suits, client dinners, promotions, and expense accounts for a world of dishes, reptiles, reading delays and math anxiety.

My life has changed in just about every way, but one.

This strengths based approach, that I learned so much about and saw making such an impact in adult learning and development, is foundational in our homeschool.

A Traditional Vs. Strength Based Approach

When I try to explain what a strength based approach to learning is I am often met with a placating nod and smile. There is a perception that spending most of our educational time on strengths, is somehow less rigorous or demanding as a traditional school environment.

More than once, I have been asked what will happen when my kids are in the "real world" and don't have their mommy around to let them do what they like to do all day long.

This is unfortunate on so many levels. It denies what research and our own experience proves to us over and over again, in favor of what we were raised to believe is the only way for us to learn.

A Traditional School Approach Weights All Subjects Equally

Think about a typical report card. The list of subjects, each with its letter grade, are all weighted equally to determine a grade point average. This average is used to determine the overall effectiveness of the student. Math matters as much as history which matters as much as science and even PE.

This approach requires the learner to focus most on the areas that are difficult and not naturally strengths, in order to avoid "dragging down the average." This means remediation and extra practice in the areas that are weaknesses.

Prior to my work with Gallup, I took this approach for granted. I assumed it was the best way.

What Gallup proved and continues to prove, over and over again, is that requiring extra work in areas that are *not* strengths might improve performance a little in those individual areas, but it does not improve the overall productivity and ability of the individual in any substantive way.

For example, a child with extra tutoring may improve that failing grade to barely passing, but the child has not really progressed in any substantive way overall.

A Strength Based Homeschool: Why It Matters

Contrast this with a Strength Based Approach

The same child would be expected to still do math, but only for short periods of time, in favor of allowing the child to spend more time in the areas that are strengths.

This mimics exactly what we do in "real life." Adults rarely pursue careers that require them to be average in everything, but instead pursue jobs in areas of interest and that utilize their strengths. For example, I am not a mechanical engineer for good reason, even though I was required to spend as much time on math throughout K-12 as someone who is.

It also bears repeating that a learner allowed to spend the most time studying in areas of strength, tends to perform exponentially better in all areas including the areas of weakness.

I think this is because the learner eventually applies what they learn more substantively in their areas of strength that the areas of weakness. For example, the child who struggles in math may naturally have a strength in science. Given enough time to pursue scientific endeavors, the child will eventually be able to apply what she's learned to math as well.

It might be the confidence it builds. It might be that the child begins to think about math differently because of the developmental and educational growth that happens in pursuing interests and strengths.

No matter what the reason, I want you to know that a strength based approach works.

Chapter 15: How to Use Strengths and Interests for Actual Learning

Endless pictures of fish stores, computer builds, reptile zoos, guitars and Harry Potter crafts - this is pretty much my Instagram feed in a nutshell.

I post these pictures because it is pretty much all I have to post (keeping it real here). I also post these pictures because they are practical examples of what strength based learning really looks like.

One of the questions I am most often asked about strength based learning is how to actually do it. It's not difficult to see the benefits for our kids, but actually implementing a strength based approach to homeschool can feel really daunting when you are first getting started.

How Do I Figure Out My Child's Strengths?

Preferred Subjects

The easiest place to start is with the subjects that are more natural for your child and the ones that produce the least resistance. For example, although my son has an extreme aversion to math, he is fascinated by chemical reactions and other scientific processes. Or my youngest, who still struggles to read basic texts but loves writing his own stories with me as a scribe.

The subjects that are natural strengths are the ones that help us begin to create and implement educational plans.

Interests

Once you have identified the traditional school subjects that are most natural for your child, the next step is to determine key interests.

For some children, this is quite simple. To give an example, anyone who comes in contact with my youngest son for more than about 45 seconds is going to hear about animals. For others this can, at first, seem difficult.

Whenever I write about interest-led learning, I inevitably hear from a mom or two who is concerned about not knowing her child's real interests.

"He only wants to play video games."

"She is really only into actresses and make-up."

"He seriously doesn't want to do anything other than watch TV all day."

I understand the hesitation – how can these interests facilitate learning?

Although I will share nitty-gritty details of how to incorporate these interests into actual learning, for now, the most important thing is to identify what they are, no matter how not-educational they may seem.

Learning Style

Finally, determining your child's preferred method and style of learning is an important component of strength based homeschooling.

Does your child prefer listening to audiobooks over reading? Does your child like to move while learning or is it more of a distraction? Do you have a child that needs to touch and feel everything?

Information about your child's learning style is critical in helping you create a plan for your strength based homeschool.

Once you have identified these three components of learning strengths for your child, you can begin to actually implement strength based learning.

Think of it like a formula – *Preferred Subjects + Interests + Learning Style = Strength Based Education*

Now, the fun and also hard part begins.

In my experience, the number one barrier to creating a strengths based homeschool has nothing to do with curriculum choices or planning. I think the biggest problem we face in taking on this approach is our own fear.

Overcoming Fear

A strength based approach typically means that we spend the majority of our time doing things that fall into the strength based formula.

Preferred Subjects + Interests + Learning Style = Strength Based Education

The question we all ask, and are afraid to hear the answer to is "What about the subjects that are weaknesses?"

It is a reasonable question, and one that forms the foundation of a traditional school approach. Most of us were taught with this mentality – the areas of weakness need remediation and the areas of strength can just be left alone. After all, they're fine. They are already getting an A in language arts. Why spend time on what isn't broken?

What helps me overcome the fear of letting go of this method, is that research has shown over and over again that spending a majority of time on our children's strengths exponentially increases their overall ability – including the areas that are weak.

More importantly, a child excited to engage in learning assimilates and retains new concepts and ideas faster and more adeptly than a child forced to achieve the average in all subjects.

Real Life Examples of Strength Based Learning

With this all in mind, let me share some real life examples of strength based homeschooling at work. This is what it actually looks like.

We went to the guitar store last week...

Four times.

We didn't buy anything. No, we walked up and down the rows of electric guitars. My son explained to me the difference between the styles, the electronics within and the various manufacturing differences.

On the way home, we listened to rock music.

Yesterday, I spent an hour with him, watching YouTube videos about building your own electric guitar, how to sand down the wood, how to install the various component parts, and how to varnish the end result.

Here's the thing – he doesn't yet play the guitar. He just wants to know all about them.

While this may seem like just an interesting hobby for an almost 16 year old boy, it is much more than that. All of this electric guitar work is an element of how we incorporate a strength based approach. I share how I use this interest to facilitate learning below - see Learner #3.

My son is not alone in this type of passion.

The following are three profiles of real children with different interests, learning styles, and strengths, with names changed for privacy.

Learner #1 – Jake

Preferred Subjects:

Enjoys science and PE

Interests:

YouTube – top 10 videos, reaction videos and anything that has to do with gamers

Video Games

Learning Style:

Auditory and Hands-on

Jake clearly has an affinity for online content and games. We have two different options for starting points in planning his learning.

Option 1: Take His Preferred Subjects and Tie-in Some Online Options

For example, if we start with science as a strength, Jake could then research different channels on YouTube that are devoted to science. Because he also has a hands-on component to his learning style, I would ask Jake to find an experiment he would like to complete online and then we would work on the project together – offline.

Or, maybe Jake could create his own Top 10 list or video about his science curriculum or fitness best practices.

Option 2: Use YouTube and Even Video Games to Teach Preferred and Required Subjects

This always scares moms a bit, and I understand why. The idea of taking a video game and allowing it to be educational is scary and unfamiliar. But stay with me here.

Start with the video game Jake loves most, no matter how much you may hate or not understand it. For example, if Jake is really into Overwatch, start there. Ask him to show you the different locations for battles in the game or have him tell you what he likes about the different characters. Once you are a but more familiar with the game, you will be able to more naturally think of ways to incorporate in actual learning. Maybe he can map the locations in the game on a real map and describes their different climates using characters from the game. Maybe he shoots his own YouTube video as if he on location and giving details about the fight (any phone works pretty well for video these days). The important thing is, meet him where he's at first.

There are also wonderful resources available on *Teachers Pay Teachers* dedicated to incorporating video games into traditional subjects including Roblox, Minecraft, Fortnite, Overwatch, to name the few that we have used, and many others.

Both of these options focus on areas of strength and learning style. Both are so much more joyful than arguing over "doing school."

Most importantly, both will allow Jake to use his strengths in a way that promotes his overall ability to master learning material. This the foundation of what research shows makes the greatest difference in our kids' overall performance.

A Word Of Caution: Jake will begin to resent and resist this approach if you try to make everything about Overwatch educational. The idea is to let him enjoy what he loves, and use it to *his* own advantage in learning, not yours.

Learner #2 – "Emma"

Preferred Subjects:

Language Arts, Music and History

Interests:

Make-up Tutorials

Fortnite

Dancing

Learning Style:

Movement Oriented

Because we covered video games in Jake's profile above, let's instead take a look at how to incorporate Emma's other interests.

Option 1: Take Her Preferred Subjects and Tie-in Her Interests

Ask Emma to explore music history, either online or through a few, beautiful books. Play various styles of music for her and ask her to pick the one she likes best. Then, together, learn a bit more about it's origins, history and key artists. Finally, ask Emma to choreograph her own dance to the song of her choice.

Option 2: Use Make-Up to Teach Preferred and Required Subjects

Make-up tutorials are very popular, perhaps Emma could create her own. Ask her to type up an outline for her video, including an intro and conclusion. You can even volunteer to be her videographer while she films.

Another option would be to find YouTube videos about the history or chemistry of make-up. She could also write an essay detailing contrasting views on femininity and womanhood, as well as how make-up can be perceived on both sides.

Both of these options focus on areas of strength and learning style. Both are so much more joyful than arguing over "doing school."

Most importantly, both will allow Emma to use her strengths in a way that promotes her overall ability to master learning material. This the foundation of what research shows makes the greatest difference in our kids' overall performance.

Again, A Word of Caution: Do not make *everything* that Emma loves into an educational experience. This is a way to invite her into learning in a more in-depth and strength based manner.

Learner #3 – "Scott" (My Oldest Son)

Preferred Subjects

Science and History

Interests

Computers and Youtube

Aquariums

Electric Guitars (recent)

Learning Style

Visual

And now we have come full circle. Scott is a pseudonym for my oldest son. He is the one obsessed with electric guitars right now. Here is how we have incorporated his strengths, both in subject matter and in interests, into his learning.

Option 1: Take His Preferred Subjects and Tie-in His Interests

My son and I went to the library and checked out a ton of books on the history of rock music and various artists. He also has been researching various methods for building and customizing guitars, including electrical components and circuitry.

Option 2: Use Guitars to Teach Preferred and Required Subjects

History and Science have been no brainers for him on this one. As such, we have also worked on incorporating language arts (NOT a natural strength) into this area of interest. He is currently working on an essay about drug abuse in rock music and doing well because he is passionate about the topic.

Both of these options focus on areas of strength and learning style. Both are so much more joyful than arguing over "doing school."

Most importantly, both allow my son to use his strengths in a way that promotes his overall ability to master learning material.

What I want you to know, more than anything else in all of this, is that creating a strength based homeschool takes a ton of time and faith. Although I have shared as many examples as possible here, the truth is, you will learn the most in trial and error with your own learner.

What I can promise you is that the research shows that this works – and not just in the areas of strength. A strength based approach teaches our children how they learn best and allows them to apply it in all subjects.

I will also promise you that a strength based homeschool can be infinitely more interesting and fun for both teacher and learner.

Chapter 16 : Teaching My Dyslexic Son to Read Does Not Always Involve Books (and other shockers!)

My youngest son is now 12 years old. He is technically in the sixth grade. He loves animals, building structures in the woods, and jumping on our trampoline as often as possible. He can do complex math in his head, complete entire science experiments on his own, and knows more about World Geography than I do.

He is also unable to read even the most basic book. He shies away from any activity that he thinks might possibly have anything to do with reading, including Sunday School, homeschool co-op classes, and has even asked me not to read aloud to him anymore at night.

My son has repeatedly said, over and over again, that he wants to learn to read, but not with books. I believe my response has always been something like, "No way Jose. We love books in this family. You have to learn to read with books."

My son is profoundly dyslexic. He wants to read – desperately. He has been asking for years to learn. *This is not about reluctance*. It is about his brain's ability to decipher and comprehend the code we call the English language. And the more he has tried and failed, the more I have researched and read books about dyslexia, and the more I have freaked out and pushed harder.

One day, as his reading lesson once again went down the path of tears, resistance, anger, and frustration, I sent my son to his room to calm down. I sighed to myself and looked down at the page he had been struggling to get through in the story book that accompanies our curriculum.

The sentences in this book were essentially along the lines of, "The six foxes jump." He is almost a teenager. He can name half the elements on the periodic table and has regularly told me all about how he would survive in the Amazon RainForest. (Between you and me, he probably could).

It struck me in that moment that my child has interests, and on some level of maturity, way beyond the books we were using to help him learn to fluidly read. It also struck me that he never resisted learning when we were using other tools (i.e. flashcards, air writing, 3D letters, etc.). It was only when we pulled out the really basic primers that he lost his mind and quit.

Could he really be on to something? What if I allowed him to learn to read without the books themselves? Would he gain back his natural joy and curiosity about reading?

More importantly, would he actually learn to read? Although everything in my heart screamed, "No way!" I decided to give it a try.

Here is what our new lessons in "reading" look like:

1. We read, but not for "reading."

Although we still read books, I read them aloud and they are not part of our dedicated time for "reading" lessons. They are books about historic figures, and age-appropriate chapter books that he enjoys. What I love is that he no longer associates books with pain and frustration. We also use wordless books. He creates stories to go along with the pictures, and he narrates them to me, using age appropriate sentence structure and vocabulary. Finally, audio books remain a regular part of his routine.

2. We use the trampoline.

We draw words on the trampoline in sidewalk chalk and he jumps to them on my prompt. We practice sight words and create sentences, without so much as a book jacket or pencil in sight. Sometimes, when reading practice is over, I will climb on with him and complete the rest of the day's learning. He thinks it is more fun sitting on the trampoline. I think it is more fun to get it done without fuss and before 1 p.m., so it works.

3. We modify the curriculum to be multisensory.

Because repetition and consistency are so important in helping the dyslexic child learn to read, we still use our All About Reading curriculum, but I modify it to allow for greater flexibility. For instance, in practicing the program's sight words, he will often say and spell the word, then tap out the letters or sounds on his forearm, then "air write" the word, and finally write the word in his notebook.

4. We incorporate my son's interests for practice.

My son loves Minecraft. He LOVES it. Did I mention he loves it? There are signs that one can create in Minecraft. It's like a blank sheet of adolescent approved paper. He asked me one day to help him write out a sentence (this never, ever happened before.) Once I realized this was an option, I decided to try and put it to good use. Now, as part of his learning, I write out a word or sentence, and he then inputs it into the Minecraft screen. Every day, we go through the signs he has created, and he practices reading the sentences. Some of them are the ones he came up with, and others are the ones I suggest, which also happen to be from the All About Reading practice list. Please smile with me and say "Win-Win!"

5. We are working our way back to actual books.

I know I need to help my son move back into practicing reading fluency. Whether he likes it or not, the best way to do this is with books. In trying to be intentional about this goal, I have started to read him age-appropriate, fun books, in which he is genuinely interested. What he doesn't know is that these books are on the reading level just above where he is currently performing. I imagine a day, in the not too distant future, when he will be able to read these same books aloud to me, without fear, shame, and frustration.

These changes have not required all that much, I am so happy to say. Our day-to-day learning is actually easier for me, now that he is not fighting it. More importantly, although I did not think it possible, my son has made more progress in the last couple of months, than in the years prior. Most importantly, he now has a sense of control, small and measured, but control just the same, over how he learns to read. It has been a learning curve for both of us, but the results have been so encouraging. There is more learning here than ever before.

Slowly but surely, he is learning to read and understand written language.

Chapter 17: Yes, It's Stressful to Homeschool a Child with Special Needs

I worked on my son's high school transcript this week.

I found myself thinking, "How did this happen? First of all, a tenth grader? What is that all about?" and then "What happened to 'I'll just homeschool them for a few years and then they can go to a private high school?'"

This same boy was the one in public school until third grade.

When I think back on that time, I remember the feeling of dread each morning. I remember the anger and frustration I felt when he wasn't getting the services he needed. I remember the fear of bullying and social maladjustment.

And I remember the intense pressure I felt all the time to find a workable solution. Homeschooling, for us, began as a way to relieve that stress and pressure.

And it did.

But the truth is, homeschooling any child brings with it a completely different kind of pressure – add special needs and learning differences into the mix, and sometimes it can be totally overwhelming.

One of the most common questions I am asked about homeschooling with learning differences is, "Isn't that a lot of pressure on you?"

The answer is yes. It is a ton of pressure sometimes.

I think this is an important topic to cover as we discuss the realities of homeschooling children with special needs. I want to give you an honest look at what homeschooling children with learning differences is really like. Sometimes it's amazing hands-on activities and sometimes it's crying in the bathroom, certain that I am messing up my children for life.

I think homeschooling brings pressure for every mom – no matter what the child's needs. But my experience has shown that there are some areas that are simply more intense for the family educating a child with learning differences.

The Pressures of Homeschooling Children with Special Needs

Educating Myself

I often hear homeschool moms of children without significant differences worrying about how they will teach math when their children are older. "What about algebra? How will I teach that? I don't know anything about it!"

This is exactly what homeschooling a child with learning differences feels like to me – but for all the subjects.

A significant part of the extra stress and pressure I feel comes from needing to educate myself so that I can educate my children. What's the Orton-Gillingham Approach to teaching dyslexic students to read? How are math drills typically accommodated in a school setting? What does the research say about executive function and learning? How do I help my sons with both?

This is just a small sample of the ongoing questions I need to answer and the reading, research, and learning I need to do before I can effectively help my sons learn.

Dealing with Doctors and Therapists

We are going to cover this in more detail in a later chapter, but I have to include it here as well. A large part of the stress I feel is, without a doubt, the many outside therapies and doctors appointments we experience. This means I am far more likely to be questioned about homeschooling, socialization, and high school far more than the average homeschooling mom.

Having to explain at best, and often defend, at worst, our decision to homeschool and the progress my boys have made because of it, is a constant stressor.

Comparison Is Awful

This is true for every single mom I know, hands down, homeschooling or not. Comparing ourselves to others is a really quick way to ruin our days.

I find that comparison, when it comes to homeschooling my children with learning differences, can be downright devastating. My heart feels like it's breaking sometimes when I look at what my friend's youngest son can do versus my own youngest. Her son is five years younger than mine and is ahead of him in school. It's the worst, isn't it?

Comparison hurts me. It hurts my son. And it brings more unnecessary pressure.

Am I Doing the Right Thing?

Again, this is a universal motherhood pressure that is aggravated by our differences. Most of the time this sounds like, "There are people more trained and with more experience in the school special education system. Am I doing the right thing? Maybe I should just let the 'experts' handle it, no matter what our experience has been."

"Am I doing the right thing?" is a loaded question around here. It inevitably brings me to the greatest pressure I feel as a mom homeschooling children with learning differences.

It's All on Me

This is the mother of all mother pressures and it takes me out sometimes. My son learning to read with profound dyslexia, executive function strategies, therapy decisions, measuring progress, and now, even high school transcripts – *they are all on me to figure out.*

At least it feels that way sometimes.

The truth is, we have an entire team of professionals that help me navigate these decisions and needs. I have a ton of support in person and online. But the "It's all on me" feeling still comes more often than I would like and the pressure it creates is never helpful.

All this pressure. All this stress. Why do this? Why homeschool at all? Because, after everything I just described, I can also tell you that it is 100% worth it.

Homeschooling is far less stressful for me and for my boys than being in the school system was for us. Yes, the pressures and stress of homeschooling children with learning differences are difficult sometimes, but I wouldn't trade the progress my sons are making and the days we spend learning together for anything.

Part Five: The Diagnoses

"Diagnosis is not the end, but the beginning of practice." -
Martin H. Fischer

Chapter 18: My Family's List of Diagnoses

I am grateful you have come this far with me.

Although I have shared little bits here and there, it seems only fair, before I get into some of the best practices for homeschooling children with specific diagnoses, that I give you a little more information about the diagnoses we work with on a daily basis around here.

Many of these diagnoses overlap. Some are fluid and may or may not be on the list once my boys are adults. But they are as much a part of our homeschool as reading and math.

In no particular order and assigned to no particular child, this is my family's list of diagnoses:

Autism Spectrum Disorder

Generalized Anxiety Disorder

ADHD

Bipolar Type 1- Early Onset

Social Pragmatic Language Disorder

Auditory Processing Disorder

Systemic Lupus Erythematosus

Sjogren's Syndrome

Learning Disorders - Reading, Written Expression, Mathematics

Common Variable Immune Deficiency (CVID)

Acute Allergic Disorder

Eosinophilic Gastroenteritis Autoimmune Disease

It hurts a little to type all of this out in one place. To see all of it, in one list, feels overwhelming.

But the truth is, this list has been powerful. These diagnoses have led us to treatment options that are working for my boys. We are making progress. I am grateful for this list.

This list has given me the freedom to do what works best for my children, especially when it comes to their education. This list is, without a doubt, why this book exists in the first place.

Chapter 19: Homeschooling a Child with Autism

I received an email from the teacher after my son's first homeschool hybrid class.

I held my breath when I opened it. Most emails back in our school days brought bad news.

"I am really looking forward to working with your son. He is quite a remarkable student. His knowledge of history is already quite impressive – not just for his age, but for anyone!"

That was it.

No concerns over his social ability or attention. No comments about his interactions with other children. No wringing of the hands because he wears crocs instead of "appropriate footwear."

Then, late last week, my son asked if he could go to the school's movie night.

"I met two boys that are really into computers and they are going to be there. They asked if I could come too."

My son made friends, immediately. He engaged in an extra-curricular activity, immediately. He is having fun and socializing *at school.*

Why am I so surprised?

The Truth About Homeschooling a Child with Autism

One of the fears we have, and the myths we believe, is that if a child is homeschooled, especially a child with autism, there is no way they will be able to "hack it in the real world", including environments with other children that are not homeschooled.

My experience has consistently been exactly the opposite.

Homeschooling my son with autism has given him the time and the grace he needed to figure himself out, before figuring the world out. It's allowed him the time and space to pursue his special interests as part of his education, instead of in spite of it.

And the fact that it is actually working, still shocks me every day.

You see, prior to my son's autism diagnosis, I used to be extremely opposed, super judgy, uninformed, and militantly against homeschooling.

I was once so rude and condescending to a homeschooling mom at the park that I wish I could go back in time and not only take it back, but clean her kitchen for her while she sips a glass of wine.

So, if you feel that same violent opposition, there is nothing but understanding and a hug for you here. It's a little crazy how much our perspectives change over the course of motherhood.

Making the decision to homeschool was not an easy one. I don't think it ever is, but <u>a</u>dding autism to the mix made it downright terrifying.

Years later, I can say that the decision to homeschool has proven to be one of the most beneficial I have made for my child on the spectrum. I would even venture to say that it has been the best decision I have made in how I approach his learning differences and special needs.

Here's why.

Homeschooling *My* Child with Autism

Individualized Approach

Because he has a genius level IQ, but also brain differences that in a school setting would classify him as "behind" means we individualize everything.

For example, my oldest is way ahead in most subjects, but struggles with holding a pencil and writing his own name. Challenging him and truly helping him learn, always requires tailoring the plan to both his level of knowledge and his sensory-motor needs. In a school setting, not only would he not be able to advance this significantly, he wouldn't have the support necessary to be able to focus on learning the subject matter, instead of struggling with the most basic aspects of the school environment.

Flexibility

With the crazy that can sometimes rear its ugly head around here, especially with <u>intense meltdowns</u> or completely sleepless, neurologically impaired nights, it has been a huge benefit to be able to tailor our days to our capabilities. On the worst days, we simply don't complete much school work. We may leave the house and head to the aquarium or call up some friends and ask if they want to come over and do a project in the kitchen or garden. When we have better days, we load up on the more detailed learning. We end up even in the end, and sometimes even ahead on our lesson plans.

Quality Friendships

In the past, I was super critical of the "socialization" part of homeschooling. I still hear it a lot. How will they be socialized? Won't they be weird? For the record, my son did not have a very "social" year in public school second grade. If anything, what he learned in a formal school environment was stay away from most other kids.

One of the greatest surprises and benefits for us have been the sweet, close friendships the boys have developed *because they are homeschooled*. When they connect with other children, there is time to get to know one another at park days or play dates or field trips. They don't interact in short snippets of recess time. They have hours to learn to get along. Because we are not changing grades and classrooms each school year, my sons have both had close friendships for three years. There is so much good that has come from this.

Here is one of the most salient examples I can share – A few years ago, my oldest was with one of his closest friends, we will call her Flower. They were outside playing with some of the neighborhood kids, when one of them came up to Flower and told her that she thought my son was "really weird" (to this day, I am not sure if my son heard her).

Sounds like a sad story, but the beautiful part comes next. Flower and her little brother, were outraged. Flower stood up to the little neighbor girl, while her brother ran into the house, went straight to his room and started crying because he felt so bad for his friend. My son had so much support and love surrounding him, that I am not even sure it registered with him the way it did for his friends.

My point is, these friendships are *real.* They don't end because of summer break, or because of the latest drama on the playground. They matter to my boys and they matter to me. I couldn't ask for a better environment in which to "socialize" my children.

Overall, homeschooling my child with autism has made the most sense for all of his needs and my own. We have learned together what works. We have maintained a close relationship. Best of all, he is taking all he has learned and applying it in real life ways that will help him as an adult.

Chapter 20: Homeschooling a Child with ADHD

We made the decision to homeschool my youngest son before he was diagnosed with ADHD.

We made the decision, in part, because we suspected it. We could see the need to move, the need to talk, and the need to ask questions (no matter who was talking) already getting him into "trouble" in more formal learning environments.

Add his reading delay and overall learning differences to the mix, and it became clear very quickly that a traditional classroom would not be ideal for my child.

Eight years later, I can look back and see the good and the bad. I can see what has worked and what hasn't. I can tell you that for my child's attention issues, beyond any other differences, homeschooling has been an excellent educational option.

Making The Decision to Homeschool a Child with ADHD

I am often asked about homeschooling children with ADHD. Most of the time, these questions come from parents tired of fighting for services and worried for their children.

Before I share our experience and what I believe to be significant benefits of homeschooling a child with ADHD, I want to say one thing up front: Homeschooling a child with ADHD is an option, but it is *not* a solution to all the problems our kiddos face and it is *not* the only way.

I know a few families just like ours, that have found excellent, more traditional schooling options and are just as pleased with the results as I am with our choice to homeschool.

The Benefits of Homeschooling a Child with ADHD

Less Administration

The truth is, homeschooling my son with ADHD does in fact, feel a lot easier than dealing with IEP's, less than supportive teachers, and the constant phone calls, paperwork, and attendance notes that I used to manage when my son was in school. If my son is having a particularly tough day, we can play outside in the morning and get some of his energy out, instead of having to bribe him to get into the car and get to school (and I don't have to worry about getting a note about the number of absences!).

Increased Movement and Hands-On Learning

For a child with attention issues, sitting still at a desk is not only difficult, it can detract from retention and overall comprehension. This is especially true for my son. If he can move or get his hands dirty while learning the subject, he is much more likely to understand and retain the learning.

This means we frequently do school on the trampoline, in our backyard, hanging upside down off the couch and standing at the kitchen table – something that is simply not feasible outside of a homeschool environment.

Timing Matters

Because we are able to easily accommodate a single learner, or even a single learner and his big brother, we are able to flex the time of day and days of the week that we study. My son has a ton of energy in the morning and is not necessarily at his best for learning. As such, we do very little structured work before 11:00 AM. Similarly, after the weekend, my son tends to be a little off (blame the change in routine and mom's very real need for coffee come Monday morning!). We do very little formal learning on Mondays and instead, use our day to complete hands-on science experiments, listen to audiobooks in the car and practice life skills like organization and planning.

Increased Confidence and Self-Awareness

This is the area that makes me most grateful for the opportunity to homeschool my child. Although my son has ADHD and a host of other learning differences, he is, for the most part, unaware of the stigma attached to these disorders. Because we homeschool, he doesn't see the reading level of all the other kids in his class. He doesn't know that he might be in a special classroom at school because of his inability to control his movements. In fact, just last week, he told his therapist that he is a very good learner. She was taken aback. She had never heard a child with so many learning delays describe himself so positively.

I told her, "He is not wrong. He is a very good learner."

He is, when he is home, learning in the ways that make the most sense for his brain and body.

If you are already homeschooling a child with ADHD, please let me encourage you that I think it matters. I think it makes a difference for our children in ways that I am only just now beginning to see and understand.

The Best Homeschool Schedule for a Child with ADHD

Consistency is essential for children with ADHD

I have heard it, read it, and been shamed by it about a thousand times over the years. Here's the thing – I know it's true. Not only do I see the benefits in my own home, but it just makes sense. When you are struggling to focus and/or transition from one thing to the next, a predictable routine decreases anxiety and simplifies decision-making.

I understand it, but creating a consistent routine and schedule for our days has not been easy. Although the need for a consistent schedule is obvious to me, it is not to my son.

In fact, most of the time, he actively resists my attempts to create a schedule that works for him. With this in mind, I want to share more about how this affects our homeschool schedule and the things that have worked best in accommodating my son's ADHD at home.

Visual and Hands-On Time Cues

Time blindness is a real thing for our kiddos with ADHD. One of my son's greatest struggles is in managing the passage of minutes, hours, days and weeks. Because of this, I have found our schedule works best when he can actually see and anticipate the transitions of the day.

We use post-its to list each task that needs to be accomplished during the day. He he progresses through the taks and/or scheduled appointments, he removes the post-it off our calendar and tosses it.

This approach is visual, hands-on and works beautiful for his needs.

Alternating Subjects

This is perhaps the best advice I can give you for managing a child with ADHD's schedule. Knowing my son's need to move, combined with his serious aversion to certain subjects, means I alternate his schedule to accommodate both.

For example, because I know reading and writing are difficult for him, I would never plan to complete them back to back. Similarly, I know he loves science and can do math in his head. With all of this in mind, our subjects usually progress like this:

1. Movement (walk the dog)

2. Reading practice

3. Hands-On Science

4. Writing Practice

5. Listen to book on Audible

6. Math while jumping on trampoline

7. History Video

8. Review accomplishments for the day

9. Movement (walk the dog)

Strengths and Interests

I have to stress the value of strength based learning again here, as it relates to homeschooling a child with ADHD. In addition to alternating my son's subjects, the amount of time we spend on each varies according to his natural strengths and interests.

For example, we may only spend 10 minutes on reading practice but will listen to his book on Audible for an hour. This focus on strengths has changed our homeschool schedule for the better.

All of these tactics are what has worked best for me and for my son with ADHD, but the truth is, the very best schedule for a child with ADHD is the one that works best for individual needs and your family's unique requirements.

For example, one mom I know schedules extracurricular classes for her son Monday through Thursday to get him out of the house and moving. It works and makes their time learning at home that much better. This would never work for my guy, but it's wildly successful because of their needs.

You know your child best. Please, try not to compare your schedule to any other. If it works, it works and that is more than enough to call it the very best.

Chapter 21: Homeschooling a Child with an Anxiety Disorder

When I was in sixth grade, I ran for student council president. One of the requirements was getting up on stage, in front of the entire school, and giving a speech about why you should be elected.

I bombed. For reals. I couldn't remember the lines I had prepared. I stuttered and started sweating. I ran off the stage as fast as I could and burst into tears. It was pretty awful.

But what I remember most about that day is what happened next. I went back to class.

I remember trying to take a math test and the page seemingly swimming before me. I remember not being able to focus on verbal directions and wondering what was wrong with me. I remember my anxiety increasing, not decreasing as the day went on.

I didn't learn a thing that day at school.

My youngest son struggles with anxiety more intense than I ever experienced at his age.

While my difficult afternoon in sixth grade ended, and school returned to normal by the next day, my son feels that same anxiety all the time. Moreover, he is struggling to learn with that same level of anxiety every day.

One of the reasons we homeschool is to <u>accommodate his learning needs</u>. But the truth is, I often struggle with my own worries when I consider how best to approach his education.

He can't just do *nothing.* He's already behind. If I don't make him do the reading lesson, he will never learn. I know he has anxiety, but at some point, we have to just do school – right?

Because of my own fears, I often find myself recreating that same afternoon I experienced at eleven years old, for my son.

"I know you feel anxious, but we need to get this done."

"Try to focus."

"This is just how school works."

I find the outcome is always the same. He struggles, gets frustrated, makes little to no progress and feels defeated. I struggle, get frustrated, see little to no progress and feel defeated.

And he retains nothing.

I have learned to just accept it, and begin to accommodate it.

Anxiety complicates my son's learning everyday.

Looking back over their early years in school and the beginning of our homeschool journey, I can see just how much anxiety affected our lives and learning.

When Your Child Is Too Anxious to Learn

It seems obvious. A child who is overwhelmingly anxious is not going to learn in a productive manner. And yet, how often do we dismiss this basic, fundamental need for safety and security in the interest of math?

My children have chronic conditions. Unfortunately, even on their best days, anxiety is a clear and present part of their lives. Because of this, through so much trial and error, we have found some ways that help them feel less anxious and help them progress in their learning.

Calm Down First

Always, always, always. No matter how much I may want to push through a project that we are working on or a book that we are reading, if my boys show signs of anxiety, I have learned that it is essential that we stop and help them calm down first.

For my oldest, this means going to the peace and quiet of his room for a bit and listening to music. For my youngest, this means getting outside and moving his body.

Only once they are feeling a bit calmer, we do move back into any learning for the day. I know this sounds simple and maybe I am just thick, but I can't tell you how many years I fought to keep us on schedule for the day instead of responding to their needs.

Learn About Anxiety

We have time built into our homeschool routine for mindfulness and behavioral exercises that help regulate mood and decrease anxiety. We have also completed workbooks together that help identify triggers, determine coping strategies, and create a common language in our home for dealing with anxiety on tough days.

Because sensory issues increase both of my boys' anxiety levels, we have started to build up a stash of calming, sensory fidgets and toys that they can reach for when they begin to feel anxious.

Focus On Strengths

Sometimes, all it takes to help one of my boys get back on track is to change the subject or topic to something that is naturally a strength. For example, if my youngest is having a tough day, rather than practicing reading, we will complete an animal study. This simple adjustment can make all the difference in diffusing increasing anxiety and helping my sons enjoy their learning.

Get Out Of The House

This is my tried and true, last-ditch, when all else fails and we all need a little break strategy. We load up the car, turn on an audio book and go for ice cream or drive through Starbucks. I drive around while they relax and listen to a good book. It counts as learning and it helps us all feel a little bit better about our day.

Let It Go

Finally, the truth is, some days we need to toss out the plan for learning and just focus on decreasing one of my boy's overwhelmed feelings. I used to feel frustrated by this, but the truth is, no learning is going to happen anyway once we get to this point. More importantly, one of the greatest benefits of homeschooling is the focus on the relationship and closeness that naturally develops. Some days, I need to just let go of all the expectations, curl up on the couch with a boy or two, and turn on a movie.

Dealing with childhood anxiety is not easy – not for mom and certainly not for the child. Add the constant presence of homeschooling and it can become messy for everyone involved. The good news is, homeschooling allows the flexibility and individualized attention that childhood anxiety craves and that helps our children feel secure.

I am so very grateful that we get to work on it together.

Chapter 22: Homeschooling a Child with Sensory Processing Disorder

Sensory Processing Disorder is actually to blame and credit for our decision to homeschool in the first place.

As you know, my oldest son was in public school until third grade. Every single day was a battle for both of us. For me, it looked like trying to get him to wear clothes that were allowed in the dress code. Socks alone were enough to make both of us cry every morning. For him, it was an all day long onslaught of noise, smells, and lighting that I know now put him in an almost constant state of fight or flight.

We made the decision to homeschool in part because sensory issues were so overwhelming for my son.

A year later, we learned about sensory processing disorder and it all began to add up. Moreover, once my son was home for a bit, he was able to share, in bits and pieces, what his school experience was like.

He could hear the sound of every single pencil writing in his 33-child classroom. He smelled the bleach used to clean the cafeteria, making it impossible for him to eat his lunch. The grass on his hands, while doing push-ups at PE, stung so much he would cry. The echo of children, lining up in the corridors and classrooms was so intense, he spent most of his time finding ways to keep his ears covered.

I had no idea how bad it was for him. Honestly, ten years ago, most of the literature about sensory processing disorder questioned if it was even a real thing. Not one professional ever mentioned it, medically, therapeutically, or educationally.

But when we began to homeschool my son, I could see the impact of sensory overload for my son more clearly.

It has changed the way we learn.

Sensory Processing Disorder And Our Homeschool

Here are just a few of the ways we accommodate my son's sensory sensitivities in our learning each day:

Dress Code

My favorite part of homeschooling in the beginning was not having to cajole my son into wearing school approved footwear. I am not kidding.

The battle for socks and shoes each day was replaced by Crocs. Crocs for play. Crocs for church. Last month, my son even chose to wear Crocs to his prom. It's a beautiful thing, not to worry or have a letter sent home again about obeying the dress code.

Both of my children struggle with clothing in general. As such, we have a lot of soft t-shirts and elastic waist shorts. It doesn't matter anymore.

Tactile Sensitivities

Holding a pencil is excruciating for my son due to tactile sensitivities. While we have worked to help him better function with this task through occupational therapy, the truth is, it's awful for him almost all the time.

The good news is because we homeschool, when it is time to learn, he can use any method of written communication he likes. Sometimes, it means he is writing with a larger, less tactile marker. Most of the time, it means he types. What matters most is *what* he is learning, not if he is using the required #2 pencil.

In addition, my son has not had to do push-ups on the grass since his school days. There are far less uncomfortable ways for him to exercise at home.

Noise Control

This was perhaps the easiest element of my son's sensory processing issues to accommodate. Simply reducing the number of children from 33 in a classroom and 300 in a cafeteria, to two at our dining room table has made all the difference in the world.

As my son has gotten older, he has been able to take in more and more noise. In fact, he now participates in a hybrid program at a local private school that does get a little noisy sometimes. Because he has the chance to rest his ears at home, he is better able to tolerate it there, and continue to learn.

Sensory Activities and Input

Perhaps one of the best things about homeschooling a child with sensory issues is that you can include sensory activities and input to help your child stay regulated.

I incorporate sensory activities into our learning as much as possible for both of my boys.

I find it makes all the difference in their level of engagement and retention in what we are learning. It also helps them stay focused and regulated as their bodies are getting what they need throughout our days.

Homeschooling a child with sensory processing disorder brings its challenges to be sure. I firmly believe it is an excellent choice, however, for a child struggling with sensory overload.

We cannot expect a child to learn when he is overwhelmed with noise, lighting, smells, and textures. Homeschooling allows us to accommodate our children in ways that help them both physically and academically.

Chapter 23: Homeschooling with the 3 D's - Dyslexia, Dysgraphia and Dyscalculia

When my youngest son was four years old, he attended a sweet little preschool Montessori program.

As part of his "graduation" to kindergarten, his teacher prepared a portfolio of his work for us to review at our last parent conference. I loved his teacher. I trusted her. She was engaged, excited to come to work with her kids each day and genuinely concerned about their well-being.

When she showed me his letter reversals and omissions, she was kind. She reassured me that these types of errors are common for preschoolers, with a kind smile. Then she carefully asked, "You mentioned a while back that dyslexia runs in your family, right?"

Eight years later, there's no question. Not only does dyslexia run in my family, but my children both have a host of learning differences that make the basics of reading, writing and arithmetic anything but basic.

It has taken all of these years to really uncover, define, and begin to understand my boys' learning differences.

For example, my oldest struggles significantly in math concepts and facts. My youngest does not. My youngest, at twelve, is barely reading at a second grade level. My oldest taught himself to read before he was three. Both of my boys struggle with the mechanics and cooperative skills in writing.

What I have learned along the way, is that these types of learning differences are not especially unusual. They are not a byproduct of a lazy child who just doesn't want to do his work. They are very real and they have names. Most importantly, there are strategies that we can use to help.

Dyslexia, Dysgraphia and Dyscalculia: What Are They Really?

Depending on who is evaluating your child, you will hear various names for the 3 D's.

Dyslexia, Dysgraphia and Dyscalculia are the terms I use to describe my sons' differences. It's what the first therapist used to effectively communicate what was going on to us and the terms just stuck.

But on all my boys' paperwork for schools and outside therapies, we use different vocabulary.

Dyslexia is also called *Specific Learning Disorder: Reading*.

Dysgraphia is also called *Specific Learning Disorder: Written Expression*.

Dyscalculia is also called *Specific Learning Disorder: Mathematics*.

According to <u>The American Psychiatric Association</u>, a person must have difficulties in at least one of the following areas, in order to be diagnosed with specific learning disorder.

1. Difficulty reading (e.g., inaccurate, slow and only with much effort)
2. Difficulty understanding the meaning of what is read
3. Difficulty with spelling
4. Difficulty with written expression (e.g., problems with grammar, punctuation or organization)
5. Difficulty understanding number concepts, number facts or calculation
6. Difficulty with mathematical reasoning (e.g., applying math concepts or solving math problems)

The symptoms must have continued for at least six months despite targeted help.

Reading problems can include difficulties with reading accuracy, reading rate or fluency, and reading comprehension. Dyslexia refers to learning difficulties related to reading.

Problems with written expression can include difficulties with spelling, grammar and punctuation, and with clarity or organization of written expression. Dysgraphia is a term used to describe difficulties with writing.

Problems with math can include difficulties with number sense, memorizing math facts, math calculations or math reasoning and problem solving. Dyscalculia is a term used to describe difficulties learning math facts and performing math calculations.

Honestly, these diagnoses helped me immensely. They helped me better understand why my children struggled so significantly, and it helped me figure out how to best help my boys learn.

Homeschooling A Child With Dyslexia

Learning to read, or rather, teaching my son to read, is the single most difficult aspect of my life as a homeschooling mom.

My son is profoundly dyslexic and twelve years old. This is our eighth year homeschooling together.

Every single school year, our number one concern, priority, stress and challenge is learning to read, without a doubt.

I try to keep it in perspective. I know that my son is so much more than his reading ability. I know that he is wicked smart and capable. I know that he is making progress and is finally able to read basic signs and the titles of YouTube videos.

But eight years is a long time to practice the top 200 sight words – for both of us.

In an effort to remind myself of how far we've come, and in an attempt to help any other moms out there struggling through the day to day realities of homeschooling a child with dyslexia, I have pulled together the following list of ideas and practical tips for helping a dyslexic child learn to read.

17 Ways To Help A Struggling Reader

In no particular order, here are my best tips and tried and true strategies for helping a child struggling to learn to read.

1. Audiobooks

This might be my favorite recommendation on this list. Audiobooks give my son access to age appropriate literature and all the beauty that comes with a wonderful story, without any concern about his reading level. Moreover, audiobooks have been a wonderful way to transition into reading chapter books. We turn on the audio and he follows along with the hard copy of the book.

2. Tandem Read-Alouds

My son really, really wants to be able to read the entire Harry Potter series on his own. For now, we sit together. I read a page and then he reads a page. It allows him to follow along with the story, even when he is intensely focused on decoding the words. It also gives him a break in-between passages that are challenging for him.

3. Change it Up

If what you are doing is not working and is adding to your child's frustration, it is 100% OK to change it up a bit. Try a different time of day, a different location (my kiddo reads best outside), and maybe even a different curriculum.

4. Hands-On Helps

When my son was first learning his letters, the best thing we ever did was buy a Montessori wooden letter set. It allowed him to manipulate and touch the letters and was essential to his ability to remember them on his own.

5. Movement Matters

My guy is a mover. He just is. Fighting it and expecting him to sit at the table for reading lessons is something I gave up on a long time ago. Now, we practice sight words with hopscotch squares and Nerf guns. I have learned that keeping his body moving allows his brain to better retain the learning.

6. Review and then Review Again

No matter how tired you are of reviewing the word 'the' or teaching the helper 'e' the truth is, your child may need more review than your reading program or your patience recommends. Periodically going back and reviewing past topics not only helps your child retain the information, it can help them feel more confident as they encounter something that is familiar and allows them to be more successful.

7. Reward Diligence

I have learned that rather than rewarding my son for learning seven sight words, I want to reward him for his hard work in practicing them. Even if he never learns the sight words, I want him to know that his attitude and approach to difficulties matters most to me and is what I think will allow him to be successful in life, no matter what his reading level.

8. Educate Yourself

If your child is really struggling and is a bit older, I highly recommend educating yourself about dyslexia and other learning differences. I found that once I knew more, I could better help my son. It also made me feel much more confident in helping him learn to read.

9. Consider an Evaluation

Along the same lines, if you are genuinely concerned that dyslexia and other learning differences are affecting your child's ability to read, I recommend looking into an evaluation. No matter what the outcome, more information about how my child learns has always been helpful.

10. Make It Fun

Games are my favorite way to review and quiz my son on reading material. Making something that can be really, really challenging for our kiddos fun, helps them relax and actually retain what they are learning.

11. Incorporate Interests

My son loves animals and rocks. We have collections of both and use them for our reading practice. We use his gemstones for sight word Bingo, we bring his lizard out and read aloud to

him, and we have a ton of books in the house about both
topics.

12. Find a Program that Works for Both of You

Finding a reading program that works for your child is great,
but it has to work for you too. I wish someone would've told
me this years ago! We use All About Reading. I cannot
recommend it highly enough, but your family may be different.
No matter what everyone else is using, find your best fit and
run with it!

13. Remember, Sometimes Slow Is the Fastest Way

It took my son 8 years to be able to read a YouTube thumbnail.
8 years.

There were times when I was so tempted to just skip ahead in
the reading program because I just couldn't do Lesson #7
again. I have learned it helps no one. If my child doesn't fully
understand a lesson, slowing down to allow him to achieve
mastery is actually faster than having to come back to it in the
future.

14. Celebrate Strengths

There are times when my son feels discouraged and less-than because of his difficulties in reading. I try to weave areas of strength into our days, around the time he is reading. This way, when he is feeling the frustration of his reading lesson, we can move into something that comes more naturally to him. It helps keep our days on track and buoys his self- perception and confidence.

15. Strew-in Interesting Books

Leaving books around the house about snakes is a trick I have employed for years. While I don't necessarily like seeing pictures of pythons in my living room, it is a seamless way to get my son reading.

16. Visit the Library Regularly

Going to the library reminds my son that books are something to be explored and enjoyed. This is important because there are times where he feels like books are the enemy. At the library, that adversarial feeling quickly dissipates as he wanders the stacks.

17. Do Something Else

When all is said and done, some days, reading just doesn't work well for my son. On the days when it starts to turn into stress and anxiety, we just do something else. We go for a walk, do a science project, or, as I have already mentioned, turn on a YouTube show about turtles. It happens and it's OK to just do something else for the afternoon.

What About Writing? Homeschooling a Child with Dysgraphia

In all my years of public school, the only bad grade I ever received on a report card was in handwriting.

I got a 'D'. Straight A's in every other subject and a 'D' in handwriting. (My cursive tends to go straight up and down, and this was back in the day where cursive wasn't cursive if it didn't slant perfectly to the right.)

I was devastated. I begged my teacher to help me improve my grade. He was kind and took pity on me. He handed me a set of worksheets with lines to practice and told me, "If you work hard and complete these, I will raise your grade for your diligence alone."

I think I cried with pure relief.

Last week, my high schooler and I once again sat down together to practice his signature. At this point, it's the only thing I require him to hand write – and even this, some days, is too much.

I am not dysgraphic. I just don't have very slanty handwriting. You can easily read what I write (most of the time). I actually enjoyed practicing my swirly signature when I was my son's age. For me, completing those worksheets in fifth grade was boring but achievable. It was simple.

For my children, however, there is no simple solution. A handful of worksheets would never be beneficial for their needs. In fact, most of the time, it would be counterproductive.

Both have dysgraphia and it is a part of how we homeschool every single day.

What Is Dysgraphia?

Dysgraphia, according to AdditudeMag.com can be described in the following ways:

"A learning disability that affects handwriting and fine motor skills.

It interferes with spelling, word spacing, and the general ability to put thoughts on paper.

It makes the process of writing laboriously slow, with a product that is often impossible to read.

When the act of forming letters requires so much effort that a child forgets what he wanted to say in the first place, it's not surprising that children with dysgraphia often hate to write, and resist doing so."

In real life, this translates into very specific and ongoing issues with writing, including basic handwriting and spacing as well as the actual ability to compose phrases and sentences in a coherent fashion.

What Does Dysgraphia Look Like in School-Aged Children?

Although this list is not inclusive, here are some of the signs of dysgraphia in school-aged children.

Illegible writing - even with no time limit given

Inconsistencies between print and cursive, upper and lower case, or sizes, shapes, and slant of letters

Unfinished words or letters, omitted words

Cramped or unusual grip, especially holding the writing instrument very close to the paper, or holding thumb over two fingers and writing from the wrist

The child talking to himself while writing, or carefully watching her hand that is writing

Slow and labored copying or writing – even if it is neat and easily read

Expression which does not reflect the student's other abilities in language and vocabulary (choosing words that are easy to write vs. words that most accurately communicate thought)

If your child is dysgraphic, you are probably nodding in recognition and agreement right now.

The truth is, most of the time, dysgraphia looks like a combination of all of these.

Homeschooling a Child with Dysgraphia: A Behind the Scenes Look

When I really stop to think about it, I realize how complex writing really is. So many things need to happen, almost simultaneously, in order for us to effectively express ourselves in written form.

We need to think of the words we want to say, recall the letters to spell them, use our hands and fingers to write them, all the while maintaining the overall thought of what we are trying to express.

Accommodations For Dysgraphia

Because of the complexity of the processes involved in writing, there are multiple accommodations that can be employed to help a child with dysgraphia – all focused on targeting a different element of the writing process.

In our house, accommodations include:

A scribe (that would be me) for ease of expression

The option to type vs. hand write almost any assignment

Extra time (in fact, as much time as needed)

Different pencils, pens and paper (For example: my oldest prefers writing with sharpie markers. The thickness of the marker makes it easier for him to control.)

These are some of the greatest benefits of homeschooling a child with dysgraphia. While these types of accommodations are available to children in school with a diagnosed disorder of written expression, they can be cumbersome and embarrassing for the child. It's a non-issue at home.

Adaptive Technology

As my boys grow older, the need to move past the constant handwriting practice and pen grips is clear. Because we are looking for independence in learning and in life, we have also started to use adaptive technology to help my youngest son.

This includes speech to text and text to speech software on his laptop. He also now has a phone that allows for speech to text in almost every capacity. He can search for items, look up how to spell words, and even text his friend, all with the sound of his voice.

Again, the advantage of homeschooling is that my dysgraphic children can employ these technological aids without any paperwork or meetings. There is no embarrassment associated with needing to use these helps.

At home, it is just simply how we learn.

Homeschooling a Child with Dyscalculia

When my son was in second grade, math was a big deal.

His class practiced timed tests every day, the same way I did 30 years earlier, as a way to increase math fluency.

The goal was simple – complete 100 basic, single digit equations in addition in five minutes. When you mastered that task, then the time decreased to three minutes. When you achieved that level of proficiency, you started all over with subtraction. Then multiplication. Then division.

(Total side note: I swear these tests increased and contributed to my math anxiety for years.)

Although we can argue all day long about the importance of these types of exercises for math fluency, please know, my son's experience with them did not end when the timer went off.

No, the rule was that a student had to stay, Monday – Thursday, and finish the test before he or she could head out to recess. For most children, this meant an extra few minutes and they were out on the playground. For my son, it meant no recess. Four out of five days a week. For the entire school year.

Try as he may, he never got past 73 out of 100 basic addition problems – not just in the timed portion, but with his *entire* 17 minutes recess added. He just couldn't master the recall necessary for all 100 problems.

At first, we blamed it on switching school districts. He went from a more progressive, conceptual based math program in first and the beginning of second grade to a more traditional, fluency based program mid-way through.

But, as time went on, it became clear that although my son was exceptionally gifted in many ways, the way he processed basic math was very, very different from the norm.

A year later, we discovered his learning differences included dyscalculia.

What Is Dyscalculia?

Dyscalculia is a specific learning disability in math. Kids with dyscalculia may have difficulty understanding number-related concepts or using symbols or functions needed for success in mathematics.

Experts believe dyscalculia is just as common as dyslexia, but a lot less is known or understood about it. It can, and often does, co-occur with other learning differences including dyslexia, ADHD and executive function deficits.

Dyscalculia often looks different at different ages. Here are some of the signs and symptoms, by age group, that may indicate this learning difference:

Preschool

- Has trouble learning to count and may skip over numbers long after other children remember numbers in the right order.
- Struggles to recognize patterns (i.e. smallest to largest or tallest to shortest).
- Has trouble recognizing and retaining numbers (i.e. knowing that "4" means four).
- Difficulty with the concept of counting. (i.e. when asked for a specific number of blocks, the child will give you an armful, rather than counting them out.)

Grade School

- Has difficulty learning and recalling basic math facts, such as $2 + 4 = 6$.
- May still use fingers to count instead of using more advanced strategies, like mental math.
- Struggles to identify +, –, and other signs

- Struggles with concepts related to math, such as "greater than" and "less than".

Middle School

- Has continued difficulty with place value.
- Has trouble with fractions and with measuring things (i.e. when baking, etc.)
- Struggles to keep score in games.
- Has trouble writing numerals clearly or putting them in the correct column.

High School

- Difficulty in applying math concepts to money (i.e. estimating the totals, making exact change and tipping).
- Difficulties with interpreting graphs or charts.
- Continued difficulty measuring things like ingredients in basic recipes.

- Has trouble applying different approaches to the same math problem.

Math freaks out a lot of homeschooling moms. I hear questions about it all the time at homeschool conferences and conventions, with or without, a learning disability.

How will I teach math?

Add dyscalculia to the mix and it can be downright daunting.

The good news is that homeschooling a child with dyscalculia can be exactly the right approach to assist and accommodate your child's needs.

Just take a look at the accommodations, typically recommended for children with specific learning disabilities in math:

Give extra time on tests.

Provide frequent checks during classwork.

It is frustrating for a student to finish an entire worksheet, only to be told that every answer is wrong and he'll need to do it again. Instead, teachers should check after every few problems. This way, a child can learn from mistakes and feel bolstered by a sense of improvement.

List the steps for multi-step problems and algorithms.

Post clearly numbered step-by-step instructions on the board, or give your student a copy she can keep at her desk.

Keep sample problems on the board.

Give students individual dry-erase boards to use at their desks.

With this tool, students can complete one step of a problem at a time, erasing any mistakes they may make.

Use plenty of brightly colored, uncluttered reference charts and diagrams.

Children with dyscalculia benefit from visual representations of math problems.

Whenever possible, allow calculator use.

Reduce the number of assigned problems.

Assigning 10 problems, rather than a full page, is enough to assess a student's understanding.

Play math games.

All of these accommodations are easily provided in a home environment. Moreover, my child is more confident in using them because he is not comparing himself to others. He never has to feel any shame in accessing the accommodations he needs to be successful.

We have also seen a significant improvement in his overall comfort level with math lessons as we have incorporated online learning into his math education.

Most importantly, homeschooling has allowed my son to complete his math education in a way that doesn't punish him for his differences. We spend substantially more time focused on his areas of strength rather than drilling him in the areas where he struggles.

I am grateful for the opportunity to help him learn in a way that works best for his needs.

This matters more to me than any timed test anyway!

Part Six: The Experts

"You may have to fight a battle more than once to win it." – Margaret Thatcher

Chapter 24: Doctors, Therapists and Moms

I sat with her, desperate for information and scared of what she might say.

It was two weeks before my appointment with the developmental pediatrician. Two weeks before I would hear the words 'Autism Spectrum Disorder' applied to my son. Two weeks before our lives changed.

I had asked her to meet me for coffee.

We had never really spent time together – we knew each other through a school program. But she knew the doctor we were seeing. She had a child with autism. She seemed to have it all figured out.

We talked for hours. She graciously shared specifics. What her days looked like. How much money can be spent on all the things for perseverations and therapies. The exhaustion. The medications. The constant nagging fear of the future, of life beyond childhood, of what happens when mom and dad aren't around.

The time I spent with this mom is one of the greatest gifts I have ever been given.

But at the time, I didn't realize it. I didn't know.

We didn't even have a diagnosis yet, much less an understanding of what our future held.

No instead, when I got home and my husband asked me how it went, I said, "I cannot believe how much time they spend in doctors' offices and with therapists. Their entire week is filled with one appointment or another. I am sure we won't have to do all that."

I was wrong.

We do all of it and more.

The sheer amount of time and energy spent on dealing with various medical professionals was what impressed me most about that conversation (at least initially). For some reason, that piece of of her life was what stayed with me.

How could one mom spend so much time dealing with so many medical professionals?

Several years, numerous diagnoses, and eleven doctors and therapists later, I know the answer to that question.

Working with doctors and therapists is part of being a mom of children with special needs – it just is.

It takes up more of my time than even homeschooling my boys.

Phone call after phone call to make appointments, confirming pre-authroizations, checking to see if the pharmacy carries this type of medicine, checking-in with insurance companies to question why the bill hasn't been paid, and being placed on the waiting lists of recommended therapists.

Waiting room after waiting room.

The endless stretch of time leading up to each appointment, rehearsing the plan for the appointment, the promise of the reward after the visit, the holding of the breath when it is time to go, hoping that he will walk to the car, get into the car, walk to the office, stay in the waiting room.

Meltdown after meltdown.

Blood pressure and weight checks, again and again.

More recommended exercises, more advice for sleeping, more admonishments about what he is eating, how much technology he is consuming, how many medicines he could be taking.

Waiting room after waiting room.

Leaving with more to do.

More to watch for and keep an eye on.

More phone calls to make.

More prescriptions to fill.

More experts to contact.

More appointments for follow-ups.

More waiting rooms.

More.

More.

More.

I recognize that all of this is not only because of my son's autism diagnosis. Add his younger brother's needs to the mix and chronic autoimmune disorders, and what you get is three times the medical crazy.

The importance of, and at times, overwhelming nature of dealing with doctors and therapists is real. It is a part of parenting a child with special needs for all of us, in one way or another.

For some of us, it is one of the most time-consuming parts aspects of being a mom.

For all of us, it requires an understanding of how to best work the system, get the optimal appointment times to avoid crowded waiting rooms, make a good impression on the therapist, organize all the medical history and test results for easy access, and learning how to appear calm through it all.

And we just don't have a ton of resources to help us through it, sadly.

All I can offer is this - we can do this. I know this is true because we *are* doing this.

The more we learn about dealing with the medical realities our circumstances require, the more we understand, the easier it gets.

And the more our children benefit.

Chapter 25: Things Doctors Just Shouldn't Say to Moms

"Where do all these diagnoses come from? Are your children adopted?"

I hung up the phone with the doctor a few minutes later and thought, "Well, add that to the list of awkward moments as a mom of children with special needs."

There have been so many questions and comments over the years that have floored me. From professionals. From folks who deal with children, and children with special needs for that matter, for a living.

While most of the doctors and therapists we work with have been and continue to be amazing, there are some comments, questions and moments that stand out as examples of what never to say to a mom of children with special needs.

If you are a mom in a similar circumstance, you are nodding your head with a knowing smile right now.

If you happen to be a medical professional, please know, I have nothing but respect for your knowledge, education, and position. I am so grateful for all you do to help families like mine every day. And might I just say, it is in your best interest to avoid these types of personal statements with a mom who slept less than three hours last night and barely got her teeth brushed in order to make her child's appointment with you.

Every single one of the following statements is from my personal experience over the last eight years.

1. "You need to try dimming the lights and no screens for an hour before bedtime."

If a mom comes in with an eleven-year-old who has several diagnoses that all affect sleep, and mentions that she feels like sleep problems might be contributing to behavioral concerns, this may not be the best response.

Out of respect for not only the mom, but every other doctor that has come before you, please don't.

Sleep hygiene is something that every single mom of a child who struggles to sleep has heard about from every single doctor since the well baby check-up at 4 weeks old.

We are well versed in sleep hygiene and best practices.

We have the list memorized.

For years we have tried to implement it and it's still not working. That's why we are bringing it up in our appointment with you.

2. "His BMI is too high. Is he drinking a lot of juice?"

No, he's taking the meds. you prescribed. Every one of them has weight gain as a likely side effect. 25 pounds in three weeks is not the result of juice. We all know it. Please, just stop.

3. "He is probably not responding to the prescription because you homeschool."

This actually happened. I was at a loss for words then, and I still am now.

4. *"If you would just make him wear shoes, he would be OK in about two weeks. You just need to suck it up for a while."*

This, after describing sensory issues that have plagued my son since birth.

This, after mentioning that wearing shoes was the number one problem my son had with going to school.

My response? *"He does wear shoes. He has to for school. But it is causing him distress. That's why I am bringing it up."*

5. *"He might need military school. It worked for my son."*

My son was eight at the time.

6. *"Your son should be kicked out of this therapy program with behavior like that."*

In a therapy program designed specifically for behavior "like that."

7. *"He is too young for a bipolar diagnosis."*

From a pediatric gastroenterologist.

8. *"If you could see his behavior on video, you would agree that he needs Ritalin."*

I am pretty sure I see his behavior all day every day.

Plus, I raised the concern about Ritalin because it has been known to potentially cause mania in children with bipolar disorder. This is not an answer. It's just mean.

9. *"If you were a warrior mom, you would be willing to try anything for your child."*

This, right before she said, *"I accept all major credit cards for my exclusive autism supplements."*

I recognize that doctors may need to cover their bases and investigate issues surrounding every one of these comments. It's not the topics themselves that create undue stress and disconnection with moms. *It's the lack of respect.*

Rather than blanket statements and assumptions, or inappropriate questions with an obvious bias, special needs moms want someone who is on their child's team. We want mutual respect, acknowledgment, and concern.

At the very least, we want someone who is going to help, and not make us feel worse. We also appreciate a little common courtesy and manners.

I think you'll find that no one is more loyal and more willing to give referrals than a mom with a medically complicated child.

We are fierce about finding good care.

We can help each other.

Please, work with us. We need you.

Chapter 26: Who Is The Expert Here?

A few months ago, my son began occupational therapy (again) for difficulties he experiences in writing.

We walked into the waiting room and saw a sweet, but very loud toddler awaiting her appointment. There were actual colorful clowns painted on the walls. All of the chairs in the room came up to my son's knees.

He's 13 years old. He wanted to bolt before the appointment, but I made him promise to at least give it a try.

30 minutes later, after me advocating for his needed service dog and being refused, his request to use a "real chair" being met with sighs and eye rolls, and an overall desire to start screaming at everyone in the place, we walked out, both of us determined to find another way.

This was a terrible example of what OT can be for our kids. My oldest son was in a wonderful occupational therapy situation for almost two full years. It changed his life. Please hear me – this is not about OT itself.

But as I share more and more about how we homeschool with learning differences and special needs, I have to say this –if a therapy is not working, it is not your child's fault. It is not your fault. You can and should make a change.

Last week, this came across my Facebook feed from a respected occupational therapy provider. It had a picture of a mug with the following print:

 Please do not confuse your Google Search with my OT Degree

In my experience, it is precisely this type of approach that causes stress and overall ineffectiveness in helping my kids.

Here's why:

I do not think it is necessary for any one individual helping a child, to establish themselves as "the expert."

In fact, I think it is counter-productive.

The best therapists and doctors are the ones who see parents as partners and equals. Yes, they have far more education and experience with a wide variety of children. That is why we spend hundreds of dollars out-of-pocket every month to see them.

But dismissing a mother doing a google search to help her child does nothing to actually help the child.

Ignoring the years and years of anecdotal data a parent can provide, in favor of a degree is dangerous for children who require an individualized, less obvious approach.

The same is also true for parents. We should never assume that our knowledge of our child is somehow the end all be all in a therapeutic equation.

No one needs to pull rank here.

The truth is, no one individual has all the expertise they need to help truly medically and behaviorally complex children.

Every single person in the equation, doctor, therapist, and parent, is an expert in their own field of knowledge.

Working with Doctors and Therapists When You Have Children with Special Needs

In my experience, collaborations built on mutual respect and reciprocity produce the best outcomes for our children.

In order to create this type of partnership with other experts, we need to choose the therapists and doctors that seem most interested in doing so.

This is the number one bit of advice I have for you today: rather than worrying about the details of the therapies, first look at the relationships being established.

What About When It's Just Not Working?

If a therapy is just not working for your child, everyone in this partnership should be aware of it and have some ownership. Too often, I think parents and even the kids themselves, shoulder the blame unnecessarily.

Sometimes, all it takes is an adjustment. For example, in my son's current OT sessions, after seeing his resistance and stress, he is working on using assistive technology rather than handwriting drills. This solution was born out of his OT's assessment of his overall ability and conversations with me about his strengths and weaknesses.

This adjustment was easy to make because we selected his OT based on both her experience and her willingness to work together. (Plus, she has a great disposition – always a plus with my youngest!)

Sometimes, however, it is time for a change. Kids grow and mature. What worked for them a year ago, may no longer be a good fit. It doesn't have to be about blame.

Working closely with doctors and therapists is one of the most important things I do for my sons. Medication management, educational therapies, and psychotherapies are only as beneficial as the strength of relationships between all involved.

Please know, if you are struggling with this aspect of parenting a child with special needs, you are not alone. I would say that this part of my life has caused more shame, stress, and tears than any other aspect of mothering my boys.

It isn't easy, but my experience has been that it is worth it to keep trying, keep investigating options, and keep working with the experts in your child's life.

Chapter 27: Just Because It Is Difficult, Doesn't Mean You Are Doing It Wrong

He threw the book and stomped off to his room.

"Don't you understand?" he yelled, clearly frustrated. "I have dys-A-lexia!" As he slammed the door, I tried to sort through a host of reactions – smiling because of the way he pronounced dyslexia, bitter because he threw the book and we have been trying to help him work on explosive reactions, sad because reading is so very difficult for him, despair because maybe we will never be able to get this right, and grateful because I know he is at least making progress, whether or not we can both see it right this minute.

He came out of his room a few moments later, sheepishly apologized and climbed up onto my lap. He rested there for a minute, and as I kissed his head and smelled his hair, I asked him what happened. The only thing he could say was, "This is too hard. I can't do it right."

Several years ago, his older brother suddenly started reacting aggressively and violent towards everyday life. He would lose it every single day, and literally destroy his room and anything or anyone else in the way. He pulled over bookshelves, punched and kicked holes in the wall, hit me in the face, threw heavy objects at my head. He stopped sleeping, preferring instead to cry and bang his head against the wall for hours and hours.

We were on several waiting lists for an evaluation. But waiting lists don't help when it's 3 AM and you have bite marks on your arms, and your baby is slamming his head over and over again into the wall.

I remember sitting next to him, rubbing his back, trying to help him settle down, praying that it would just stop, and saying to myself, "This is just too hard. I can't do it right."

When we finally got the diagnosis, I distinctly remember asking the developmental pediatrician what I was "doing wrong" in caring for him. Her answer was so simple.

"Just because this is hard, doesn't mean you are doing it wrong. It's going to be difficult. It is difficult. There is no way around that. But it doesn't mean you are doing it wrong. Sometimes things are just hard."

I know my son and I are not alone in feeling this way. So many of us want to know how we can fix it, what we aren't doing, what's the right way. The truth is, sometimes it is just hard. Sometimes the difficulty level in this game called life is way beyond any of our abilities. It doesn't mean we are doing it wrong.

I gathered my frustrated boy up in my arms, carried him back over to the table with the books and the flashcards and pencils, and I sat down with him. I asked him to face me, looked him straight in the eyes and said, "Just because this is hard, doesn't mean you are doing it wrong. But we don't quit. When something is this important, no matter how difficult, we keep going. Even when we get frustrated. Even when we are sure we can't take it anymore."

Even when we know that we are in way over our heads and have no chance of ever not being faced with this circumstance. We take the next step.

And then the next.

And then the next.

Chapter 28: When Mom Is Depressed

It's been coming on for a while now.

And with good reason.

The list of diagnoses and medicines. The boys' meltdowns and anxiety attacks. The constant hypervigilance. The lack of sleep. The loss of any real personal time.

And the intense grief that my youngest is spinning out of control in a mood disorder that has taken over his mind.

This time it didn't sneak up on me. No.

This time, depression has hit me like a freight train.

It's important that I say it out loud.

I'm battling depression. For reals. Like with boxing gloves and a mouth guard. Naming it matters. It gives me back just a little bit of control.

Some days are easier than others. I can get out of bed and do all the things for all the people who rely heavily on me to do all the things. Some days I just want to cry and pull the covers up over my head.

Part of it is chemical, I know it. I see it in my family history and even more so, in my own. Most of it is the loss of ordinary – the grief that my sweet son is being taken over by illness and I cannot stop it.

The Reality of Depression and Mothering a Child with Special Needs

I am depressed and it's hard.

And I know I am not the only one.

Maybe you are too. Depression and motherhood happen at the same time, for so many of us. Depression and mothering a child with special needs? Perhaps even more so.

Please hear me – you are not alone.

You are not the only mom who struggles just to make it through another day. You are not the only mom who worries about how to care for herself, while at the same time care for her children. You are not the only mom taking prescription medication, or in therapy, or both.

And I want you to know that, although I am depressed, I am not without hope. I have been here before. I am sure I will be here again.

Depression takes time to heal – just like any other illness.

Today, that looks like letting go of the laundry and taking a walk instead. It's having another cup of coffee and curling up with a book. It's going to bed early. It's asking my husband for help and accepting my friend's offer to grab dinner for us.

It's praying the "Help me, please" prayers and the "I can do all things through Him" prayers. It's a nap, if and when I can get one. It's just doing the minimum, and more importantly, *not* beating myself up for it.

I will give myself the same grace I extend to my children when they are struggling. And I will remember that taking care of me, is an essential part of being a mom.

Taking care of me *is* taking care of them.

Chapter 29: The Very Best Advice I Can Give You for Homeschooling a Child with Special Needs

I began watching a docu-series on YouTube last week, all about different families raising children with varying special needs. The single mom with three kiddos on the spectrum. The 18 year old girl with significant learning disabilities trying to find a job. The elderly dad caring for his 49 and 46 year old children, wondering what will happen to them when he is gone.

I cry every episode. I laugh every episode.

Most of the time, I find myself nodding in agreement, in understanding and in support of the decisions these families are making to live as well as possible. After a week of these videos, there is one thing that stands out – no matter what the disability or difference, no matter what the gender of the primary caregiver, no matter what the level of daily care required – these families are happy.

They are happy and they are doing the very best they can.

As I end our time together here in this book, I find myself thinking of them:

The adult children, desperate to find their place in a world that seemingly doesn't seem to want them.

The parents fixing the lunches just so, because they know a meltdown isn't necessary over a cracker.

The dynamics that seems so familiar to me, but to an outsider watching, might look a lot like coddling or just plain weird.

As I consider what I have learned, I realize there is one common thread that exists across all of our lives.

We are all doing whatever we need to do to make our lives work.

The Very Best Advice I Can Give You For Mothering a Child with Special Needs

I am often asked what advice I would give a mom new to her child's diagnosis. The longer I have been a special needs mom myself, and the more diagnoses my children have received, my advice has changed a bit over the years.

Almost a decade in, this is the very best advice I can give you:

Do Whatever Works.

It may seem simple, but if you are living this life every day, you know better. If you are mothering a child with special needs, you know how different and overwhelming life can be. Making the choice to do whatever works can be downright terrifying.

Doing whatever works for your family means letting go of your own expectations for how it should be, how you want it to be, and how you thought it would be.

Doing whatever works means letting go, even when it feels like your life is already spiraling out of control.

It means judgement from other parents, even other homeschoolers, who don't understand - who couldn't possibly understand.

It means questions and confused looks from doctors and therapists who don't have as much experience as you do with your kiddos.

Doing whatever works means you will question yourself all the time.

Am I letting him get away with too much?

Am I being unreasonable?

Am I ruining my child?

All of this is true, and yet the best advice I can give you is still the same.

You need to let go and do whatever works.

It's a paradox to be sure, but it's true. When we finally let go and lean into the life we have been given, as much as it may seem like we are giving up so much, this is when we finally have a bit of freedom and control.

Whatever works is what allows us to enjoy our lives and our children again. It frees us to be parents again, not just caregivers and teachers. It's not easy, but I can tell you that when I finally let go, I found so much to be thankful for. I found a life I was willing to embrace, instead of fight.

My children are better for it.

I am better for it.

About The Author

Shawna Wingert is a special education teacher turned writer, speaker, and consultant. She is also a homeschooling mom of two brilliant boys with differences and special needs. Shawna has written three other books for parents of special needs – Everyday Autism, Special Education at Home and Parenting Chaos. She has also been featured in special needs discussions on Today.com, The Mighty, The Huffington Post, Autism Speaks, Weird Unsocialized Homeschoolers and Simple Homeschool.

You can find Shawna with her voice actor husband and two wonderful boys in Southern California and online at NotTheFormerThings.com.

Printed in Great Britain
by Amazon